CULTURES OF THE WORLD

NEPAL

Jon Burbank

MARSHALL CAVENDISH
New York • London • Sydney

Reference edition published 1993 by
Marshall Cavendish Corporation
2415 Jerusalem Avenue
P.O. Box 587, North Bellmore
New York 11710

© Times Editions Pte Ltd 1991

Originated and designed by
Times Books International
an imprint of Times Editions Pte Ltd

Editorial Director	Shirley Hew
Managing Editor	Shova Loh
Editors	Goh Sui Noi
	Leonard Lau
	Roseline Lum
	Siow Peng Han
	Tan Kok Eng
	MaryLee Knowlton
Picture Editor	Y.M. Kaung
Production	Edmund Lam
Art Manager	Tuck Loong
Design	Ang Siew Lian
	Lee Woon Hong
	Ong Su Ping
	Katherine Tan
Illustrators	Kelvin Sim
	Cherine Lim
Cover Picture	Dominic Sansoni

Printed in Singapore by Times Offset Pte Ltd
Bound in the United States of America

Library of Congress Cataloging-in-Publication Data
Burbank, Jonathan, 1951–
    Nepal / Jonathan Burbank.—Reference ed.
       p. cm.—(Cultures of the World)
    Includes bibliographical references and index.
    Summary: Explores in pictures and text the cultural
history and religious practices that still pervade
everyday life for the major ethnic groups that inhabit
this remote and fascinating mountain country.
    ISBN 1–85435–401–9
    1. Nepal—Juvenile literature. [1. Nepal.]
I. Title. II. Series.
DS493.4.B87 1991
954.96—dc20   91–15866
                                                  CIP
                                                  AC

INTRODUCTION

IF PEOPLE KNOW ABOUT NEPAL at all, they know it as the home of Mount Everest, the world's tallest mountain. The Himalayan mountains that stretch across Nepal's northern border contain eight of the 10 tallest mountains in the world.

The mountains that cover over 80% of the country are certainly Nepal's best known feature, but they are not the whole story. Nepal is the birthplace of the Buddha, founder of one of the world's greatest religions. Nepal is also an important pilgramage site for Hinduism, South Asia's other great religion.

Living on Nepal's mountain sides and in its narrow valleys are dozens of different ethnic groups, speaking different languages, worshiping different gods, and living in different cultures. Somehow, all these different groups have lived together in peace, even though Nepal is one of the poorest countries in the world.

This book acquaints us with a country which is not very well known, but well worth learning about. It is one of the series, Cultures of the World, a look at people and their lifestyles around the world.

Kathmandu

CONTENTS

This Tamang man comes from one of the many hill tribes in Nepal. The Tamangs often come down from their homes in the hills to Kathmandu Valley in search of work.

CONTENTS

In the higher areas, a great deal of domestic life takes place on the roof top of houses. It's the best place to dry crops and to bask in the warm sunshine.

GEOGRAPHY

MILLIONS OF YEARS AGO, the world was one big landmass called Gondwanaland. Gondwanaland came apart and its pieces drifted through the ocean. As the years went by, the pieces of the landmass drifted further and further apart and the waters which divided the land became today's oceans and seas. The landmasses were broken up to form huge continents and tiny islands scattered all over the globe.

The story of Nepal began about 10-15 million years ago. Then, present-day India was separate from the continent of Asia. But earth movements pushed India closer and closer till finally it collided with Asia. The force which followed the meeting of two landmasses pushed the land up, forming majestic mountains and hills. And Nepal was born.

Today, Nepal is a landlocked country, surrounded by China in the north and India in the south. It has a total area of 56,139 square miles with a population of 18 million people.

Although 85% of Nepal is mountainous, it can be divided into three geographical regions: the towering peaks and range of Himalayas, the cool terraces and valleys which form the Middle Hills, and the warm, humid lowlands of the *terai*.

Opposite: **Nepal is home to the Himalayas, the tallest and youngest mountain range in the world.**

Below: **The subcontinent of India used to be part of South Africa, Australia and the Antartica. The movement of the earth's crust over millions of years has pushed it apart to fuse with the Asian continent.**

Along trade routes in the mountains, caravans of horses are used to transport goods from one town to another. The steep and rugged geography of Nepal makes it very difficult and impractical to build roads.

THE HIMALAYAS

"Himalaya" comes from two words in Sanskrit, one of the oldest languages in the world. *Hima* means snow and *alaya* means abode. This is not surprising as the Himalayan mountains are covered with snow throughout the year. The range stretches across the whole northern part of Nepal.

About 33% of Nepal is at altitudes over 10,000 feet. About 10% of Nepal's population lives here, subsisting as traders, herders and farmers. Few crops can grow here: barley, millet and potatoes are the main ones. These grow up to about 14,000 feet.

The climate is very cold with heavy snowfalls, especially in winter. There is less oxygen in the air and people arriving from the lowlands will have trouble breathing. Some people develop altitude sickness, which can kill unless they go back to a lower altitude.

MOUNT EVEREST

In the entire world there are only 14 mountains over 26,247 feet, and eight of the 10 highest ones are within Nepal, including Mount Everest, the highest mountain in the world at 29,028 feet (see picture).

Different mountains were thought to hold the title as highest in the world. At different times Dhaulagiri, Kanchenjunga and Gauri Shankar (a tall mountain visible from the Kathmandu Valley) were all thought to hold the crown.

Everest was not confirmed as the highest mountain in the world until 1863, after a survey done by the Indian Survey Office (at that time, India was ruled by Britain). On the Tibetan side, it is called Chomolungma, and on the Nepali side, Sagarmatha. Both names mean "mother of the world." The survey, unaware of these names, first called it Peak 15 and then, Everest, after a former head of the survey office.

Everest remained unclimbed despite numerous attempts until Sir Edmund Hillary and Tenzing Norgay Sherpa finally climbed it in 1953. Rheinold Messner and his partner Peter Habler were the first to climb it without using bottled oxygen in 1978.

In the mid-80s, Everest's position as the highest mountain was challenged when a geographer claimed that Mount K-2 in Pakistan was higher. Measurements using lasers and satellites confirmed Everest is the highest, even higher than at first thought.

A typical village in the Middle Hills. Terrace fields have been carved out of the hillsides for growing rice, barley, beans and millet.

THE MIDDLE HILLS

Fifty percent of Nepal is an area called the Mahabharat Range or the Middle Hills. About half of Nepal's population live here. Calling them hills is a little deceiving, because almost anywhere else in the world they would certainly be called mountains.

The tops of these hills vary from about 5,000 to 12,000 feet (Mount Whitney, the highest point in the continental United States, is 14,494 feet tall). Seen from the air, the area is a series of endless steep ridges. Over the centuries, steep terraces for growing food have been built wherever possible.

The rugged landscape makes motor roads almost impossible to build. Nepalese almost always travel by foot. Distances are not measured by miles, but by the hours or days it takes to walk to a destination. Anything for sale in the meager stores, the few books in school and the scanty medical supplies, comes in on the backs of men, women and children.

The Middle Hills

The Middle Hills, once crowned with thick luxuriant forests, are becoming more and more barren. Villagers depend on the forests for fodder, firewood and building material. Increasing population has forced them to cut trees faster than they can be replaced. Unfortunately, the loss of foliage causes village water supplies to dry up and soil erosion eats away at the hillsides.

There are several large valleys scattered among the hills. The largest one is the Pokhara valley in central Nepal, while the most famous one is the Kathmandu Valley, 124 miles to the east of Pokhara.

Ask someone in the Middle Hills traveling to Kathmandu where he or she is going and the answer may be, "Nepal." For many people, Kathmandu is Nepal.

A picturesque Nepalese village. Life in the village, though, is very difficult. There are no telephones, health clinics, electricity, running water and other modern facilities.

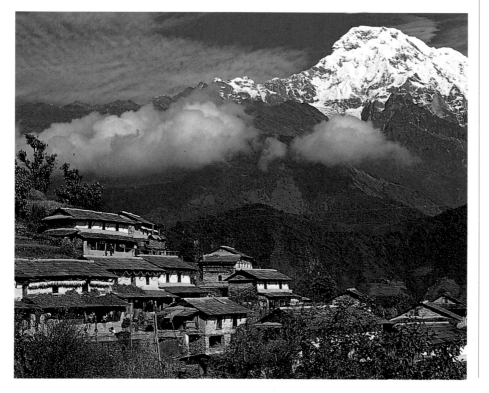

THE KATHMANDU VALLEY

The Kathmandu Valley has always been the heart of Nepal. It is not very large, about 450 square miles, and now is home to about 1,000,000 people.

The valley lies at almost the exact latitude of Tampa, Florida, but its elevation of 4,368 feet gives it a mild climate. Temperatures rarely go above 86 F in the hot season and even in winter, daytime highs are about 62 F.

The city of Kathmandu, the kingdom's capital, has a population of over 300,000 people and is also home to the king and queen of Nepal. It was founded by King Gunakamadeva in the 10th century. The name Kathmandu was derived from a temple within the city called, Kasthamandap, built in that same century.

THE TERAI

The only flat part of Nepal is a narrow strip along its southern border with India. It is called the *terai*. Because it forms part of the flood plain of the Ganges River in northern India, the *terai* is very fertile.

However, it used to be uninhabitable because of malaria, a disease spread by mosquitoes. In the 1950s, the World Health Organization (WHO), sponsored a program to spray large tracts of the *terai* with a pesticide known as DDT. The malaria was brought under control and the Nepalese government encouraged settlement of the area by hill people. The *terai* quickly changed into Nepal's bread basket and rice bowl. It is also the center for what little industry Nepal has.

Today, the *terai* is home to over 40% of the population although it forms only 15% of Nepal's land area. Every year, people from the Middle Hills are migrating here at an increasing rate.

The climate in the *terai* is extremely hot, with temperatures in the summer (April to June) reaching 100 F. A deadly wind called the *loo*, with temperatures of over 112 F, sometimes kills people in their fields. The heavy monsoon rains from June to September bring cooler temperatures and the rains for the rice fields.

Although the *terai* grows much of Nepal's rice, there has been little mechanization by farmers and animals are often used to plow the land.

The melting ice from snow-capped mountains form the source for many of Nepal's rivers and streams.

RIVERS

Nepal has thousands of streams flowing off its mountains and hillsides into hundreds of rivers. They rush down along rocky riverbeds, forming rapids and spectacular washes of whitewater. Yet out of those hundreds of rivers, only three are strong enough to cut through the Middle Hills down to the *terai* and on to the dusty plains of India. There is the Kosi in the east, the Kali Gandaki in the center and the Karnali in the west.

In the monsoon, the rains swell the rivers to many times their normal size. There are few bridges and many of them are washed away by the waters. Flooding rivers can wash away houses, even whole villages.

The rivers are often called Nepal's only natural resource. No one argues that there is tremendous hydroelectric potential, but building and maintaining hydroelectric plants in Nepal's rugged landscape is more difficult and expensive than anyone imagined. That raises the cost of the electricity produced, making it too expensive for the Nepalese.

VEGETATION

The extremes of altitudes in Nepal create many different climates and environments which result in a fascinating variety of flora.

In the *terai*, for example, a hardwood, sal, is the dominant tree and provides excellent timber for building and furniture.

In the Middle Hills there are pines, alders, oaks, hemlock, and forests of evergreens, junipers and birchs. There are also many forests of large rhododendron trees in the east and center of the country.

The bright red blossom of the rhododendron tree is Nepal's national flower. One of Nepal's most beautiful sights are the forests of rhododendrons in bloom, turning whole hillsides red in the spring.

Nepal's forests provide over 85% of all the energy used in the country. The trees are also used in all types of construction and the leaves provide fodder for the farmers' livestock.

The rapidly growing population is using up the forests faster than they can be replaced. One report says 3% of the forests are disappearing every year. Each year, as more and more hillsides are being striped bare, the soil on the hills is washed away in the monsoon rains. Without the fertile topsoil, nothing can be grown on the hills.

Saving and replanting lost trees is taking place, but it takes a generation to replace what is lost in a day. Deforestation is growing and many consider it the most critical problem facing Nepal.

The rhododendron blossom is the national flower of Nepal. The trees can be found even at 9,000 feet, though the higher they grow the later they blossom.

Yaks are beasts of burden in the Himalayas. If they travel below 7,000 feet, they get sick and can sometimes die.

ANIMAL LIFE

In the remaining jungles of the lowlands, especially in the national parks, are Bengal tigers, rhinoceroses, leopards, huge buffaloes, bears, monkeys and all kinds of smaller mammals. You can also find two species of crocodile. Gharials have a needle-nosed snout and will only eat fish. Muggers have big snouts and can be 10 feet long. They will eat anything.

Nepal's most famous and reclusive resident is the rare snow leopard. Little was known about these beautiful silver and black cats until recently. They are very solitary, shy and live in the high Himalayan region.

There are ongoing conservation programs to rebuild the populations of tigers, rhinos and ghairals, which were threatened with extinction. But not everyone is in favor of the conservation programs.

Farmers suffer terrible damage from these animals. Tigers and leopards eat livestock and occasionally a human. Rhinoceroses can ruin a farmer's entire crop in one night. A troop of monkeys will eat through a field in an hour. So it comes as no surprise that most Nepalese feel they are competing with the same animals others are trying to save.

16

THE YETI

Nepal's most famous resident, the *yeti* (also called the Abominable Snowman) may not exist at all. The Sherpas, who share its habitat, call it the "yet-tch" and have even distinguished two different types: one type that eats cattle and another that eats people.

The *yeti* was dismissed as a legend until a Major Waddell found footprints in the snow in 1899. In 1921, the leader of an Everest expedition reported seeing a dark creature walking in the snow and found some strange footprints.

The *yeti* has managed to elude discovery despite numerous expeditions sent to capture him. The famous mountain climber, Eric Shipton, found a set of footprints in 1951, which prompted several expeditions, including one led by Sir Edmund Hillary, the first conqueror of Everest.

A supposed *yeti* scalp was taken from the Pangboche Monastery for tests, and identified as belonging to a mountain goat. Photos of *yeti* footprints were found to be small bird and rodent tracks which melted in the sun.

Interest in the *yeti* died down after those disappointments, but when a Sherpa woman was allegedly attacked by one and several of her yaks killed in 1974, interest rose again.

What does a *yeti* look like? Tall, maybe taller than a man, covered in orange fur with a pointed head— some reports say its feet point backwards. One theory is that it's a giant orangutan species that was thought extinct. Until we actually find one the *yeti* will always remain a mystery, but there is certainly no reason why it couldn't exist.

HISTORY

NEPAL'S EARLY HISTORY BEGINS in the Kathmandu Valley. It has become a mixture of fact and legend. The fact is the valley was once a huge lake. Legend has it that the god Manjushri sliced the valley wall at Chobar (where there is a narrow gorge) and drained the water. Geologists tell us the lake drained somehow about 200,000 years ago.

The Hindu god, Indra, is said to have visited the valley of Kathmandu in the 7th or 8th century B.C. disguised as a human and met with the king. Siddharta Gautama, the founder of Buddhism, was born about 563 B.C. in Lumbini, a town located on the plains of the *terai*. He is also believed to have visited Kathmandu during his wanderings.

Though much of the country's history is shrouded by myths, it is certain that by the time of Nepal's first golden age during the Licchavi Dynasty around A.D. 300, the influence of Hinduism and Buddhism had been firmly entrenched in its society. During those years, visitors from the Chinese kingdom marveled at the architecture and richness of the king's palace and courtyards. When the last Licchavi king died in A.D. 733, Nepal plunged into the dark ages of history.

Opposite: **The splendor of medieval Nepal reflects a history of rich cultural traditions and advanced architectural achievements.**

Above: **A portrait of King Prithvinarayan. He is known as the "Father of the Nation" because of his military conquests which united the warring states of Nepal.**

THE GREEN TARA

One of the most significant legacies of Nepal was its introduction of Buddhism to Tibet. A Nepalese princess, Bhirkhuti, was given in marriage to the powerful Tibetan king, Tsrong Gompo.

The man she was sent to was the strongest, fiercest warrior of his day. He and his army were so feared even the powerful Chinese sent another princess in marriage as a sign of respect. Bhirkuti's faith proved strong enough to convert the king and Tibet to Buddhism.

Today, Bhirkuti is still loved in Tibet and worshiped as the Green Tara, symbol of mercy and compassion. She is also worshiped by Buddhists in Nepal.

The pagodas of Patan. In the 16th century, Patan was one of the four rich kingdoms occupying the Kathmandu Valley.

THE MALLAS

In 1200, the Malla Dynasty was established. Although the early Malla kings were strict Hindus, they established a tradition of peaceful co-existence with Buddhists which is still strong today. They were also strong administrators who strengthened and codified the caste system.

For the first three centuries, the valley faced many invasions from western Nepal and Moslems from northern India. There were as many as 80 small kingdoms in what is now Nepal, all fighting and bickering to increase the size of their tiny kingdoms. Moslems from Bengal did actually overrun the valley in 1364. However, the Mallas regained control within a week, and the Moslem occupation of the kingdom failed to leave behind any lasting influence.

The Mallas in the Kathmandu Valley prospered and Nepal's second golden age began in the 15th century. The valley's three main cities: Kathmandu, Bhaktapur and Patan grew wealthy on the trade between India and Tibet. Most of the sculpture, woodcarving and buildings the valley is famous for today were built during this time.

Yaksha Malla was the greatest of Malla kings, putting together a kingdom far bigger than the present size of Nepal , but his kingdom was

divided among his four children. Their quarrels and bickering fragmented the small Kathmandu Valley into four kingdoms. Over the next 200 years, each kingdom built fine temples and palaces, but their rulers (all cousins), schemed against each other and eventually caused their own downfall.

THE HOUSE OF SHAH

Sixty miles west of Kathmandu, Prithvinarayan Shah, king of the small Rajput kingdom of Gorkha, watched the bickering of Kathmandu's petty kings and decided to strike. He was brave, a born leader, a good strategist and a good politician. He was also very persistent: it took him more than 20 years to triumph. Fortunately for him, even after he entered the valley the Malla kings refused to join together. Through battles and political intrigue, Prithvinarayan Shah conquered the valley's kingdoms one by one. In 1768, he became sole king of the valley.

He and his successors expanded the kingdom until Nepal included Sikkim in the east and touched Kashmir in the west. By the early 1800s, Nepal was one of the greatest powers in South Asia.

Prithvinarayan Shah's castle in Gorkha. It was from this hilltop fortress that he began the conquest of Kathmandu Valley.

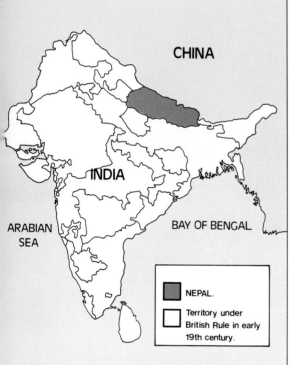

The British occupation of India in the early part of the 19th century.

NEPAL.

Territory under British Rule in early 19th century.

THE BRITISH

Nepal's expansion brought it into contact with the other expanding power of the time—Britain. In 1814, they went to war over a territorial dispute. After some initial Nepalese success, the British prevailed. The treaty of 1816 reduced Nepal to almost its present size and gave Britain the right to keep a representative in Kathmandu.

Forced by the treaty to let the British have a representative in Kathmandu, the Nepalese gave him the worst land in the valley, full of malaria and "evil spirits." They also denied him the right to leave the valley except to go to and from India by a single route.

Nepal was so resentful of foreigners it closed its borders until 1951.

THE KOT MASSACRE

The defeat by the British threw Nepal into a turmoil. Members of the aristocracy had inherited powerful armies without being able to extend their territory. So factions among the aristocracy were formed and they turned against each other in a political struggle to control Nepal.

In 1847, the queen's lover was murdered in a palace intrigue. The furious queen gathered the various squabbling factions together in her palace and accusations flew. Hands went to swords and, by morning, several dominant families were wiped out. Jang Bahadur Rana, one of the faction leaders, survived.

Rana appointed himself prime minister and he and his family virtually

Jang Bahadur Rana was the first Nepalese leader to travel to England and France in 1850. His family then continued to rule Nepal for the next 100 years.

ruled Nepal for the next 115 years. The king was reduced to a mere puppet on the throne. The Ranas did nothing to improve the country and the lives of the people. For example, when the Ranas were overthrown in 1951, only 5% of the population knew how to read and write.

THE RESTORATION OF MONARCHY

After India's independence in 1947, pressure grew in Nepal for the Ranas to reform the government. There were even protests and strikes at factories in the *terai*. The opposition was led by the able and charismatic B.P. Koirala, who operated from a base in India. But suddenly in 1950, the king decided to seize the initiative by escaping from his bodyguards. He sought refuge in the Indian Embassy and requested for asylum.

King Tribhuvan was flown to India and he demanded the Ranas return power to him and the people of Nepal. The Ranas responded by declaring his crown null and void, and appointed Tribhuvan's infant grandson king. All governments refused to recognize the new king and expressed their support for Tribhuvan.

The king and queen toss coins to dancers at a festival. Presently, the monarchy functions only as the figurehead of Nepal.

Tribhuvan declared the support for a democratic government. He became a rallying point for all Nepalese against the Ranas. Popular support for the king soared and within a year he had taken control of Nepal. King Tribhuvan laid the foundation for parliamentary democracy before his death in 1955. In 1959, a constitution was adopted and all political power was transferred from the king to an elected government.

DEMOCRACY AGAIN

The Nepal Congress Party came into power. But in 1962, after constant friction between the king and cabinet, Tribhuvan's son, King Mahendra, forcibly dissolved parliament with the help of the armed forces.

Mahendra and his son, Birendra, ruled Nepal with almost absolute power. All political parties were banned. Fundamental rights of free speech and press were restricted. Local and national legislative bodies were rubber stamps for the king and his representatives.

In the spring of 1979, discontent led to riots in Kathmandu and the *terai*. The king agreed to hold a national referendum on whether to have

a multiparty system or not. The results of the referendum were contested, but the king won by a narrow majority.

Yet, little economic progress was made and many people remained poor and oppressed. Corruption was rampant among public officials.

In 1990, discontent could no longer be contained. After a series of bloody battles between demonstrators and police in which hundreds of citizens were killed, the king was forced to give up most of his power to a democratically-elected, multiparty parliament.

The Ranas used the wealth of Nepal to benefit themselves by building palaces and living a life of luxury. This Rana palace has since been converted into a college dormitory.

25

GOVERNMENT

DURING THE YEARS from 1959 to 1962, Nepal enjoyed a brief spell of democracy. However, disputes between the monarchy and cabinet led the king to dissolve parliament and amend the constitution to obtain absolute power. The Kingdom of Nepal underwent dramatic changes again in 1990, when the ruling monarchy under King Birendra was forced to legalise political parties. An interim government was also set up to run the country until free elections was to be held in 1991.

ADMINISTRATIVE ORGANIZATION

Nepal is divided into 14 *anchal* (zones). In the east and far west, these zones are narrow and run from the southern to the northern border. This means that each zone contains a chunk of the Himalayas, a large slice of the Middle Hills, and a sliver of the *terai*.

Each zone is further divided into a number of *jilla* (districts). There are a total of 75 districts in Nepal. Each district is divided into nine blocks called *ilaka*. The *ilaka* are divided into *panchayat*.

The *panchayat* is traditionally the smallest unit of organization. In modern times, each *panchayat* has been further divided into nine wards. In the sparsely settled far west, a ward may be just a dozen households.

Each *panchayat* elects a Pradan Panch who acts like the village or town mayor. People also vote for members of the district assembly called the Jilla Panchayat, and the members of the national legislature called the Rastriya Panchayat.

Nepal's government has always been highly centralized. Local districts and *panchayat* have very limited powers to pass local legislation or raise money. The central government in Kathmandu has always kept strict control over not just legislation, but also (and more importantly) the distribution of Nepal's meager budget.

"Nepal is like a yam between two boulders [China and India]."
—*Prithivinarayan Shah*

Opposite: **The Nepalese flag is shaped as two pennants, with the sun and moon on the top pennant and the sun alone on the bottom pennant.**

Civil servants in Nepal wear the *dara–sarwal*, the traditional male suit beneath a Western-style jacket.

PEOPLE POWER

Except for the brief democratically-elected prime ministership of B.P. Koirala in the early 1960s, Nepal has always been governed by a strong figure who came to power by birthright or force or both. The king *was* the government. Everyone was ultimately answerable to the king; the king had only himself to answer to.

Pro-multiparty democracy demonstrations started in early 1990 after the people were inspired by the revolutions of eastern Europe. The demonstrations gained momentum quickly in the major urban centers and, at one point, government offices were abandoned as civil servants joined the protesters in a march near the palace.

The government tried to put down the opposition but, even when the police fired on demonstrators, the protest marches grew bigger the very next day. When dozens of protesters were killed as they approached the palace, the demonstrators threatened to become violent, too. The government was almost paralyzed by the time the king went on the radio in late April and agreed to give up power and allow the establishment of a multiparty government.

After tense negotiations where the monarchy tried to maintain control in the name of national unity, King Birendra finally agreed to the new constitution which called for a freely-elected parliament. The prime minister is chosen from the political party in control of the legislature. The two main parties are the Nepal Congress and a coalition of seven communist parties.

With democracy comes political rallying. Here the members of the Marxist-Leninist party parade the streets.

FREE ELECTIONS

In May 1991, Nepal held its first multi-party elections in 32 years. Four main political parties contested for seats in the 205-seat House of Representatives: the moderate Nepali Congress party which came into power at the last elections in 1959, the United Marxist-Leninist party (UML) which represents the communists and two monarchist parties, both of which are called the National Democratic Party.

The majority of seats were won by the Nepali Congress party who will form the next government of Nepal. The communists came in a strong second, and look set to form a strong opposition in parliament. After so many years of hardship and poverty, Nepal's new government is expected to face tremendous pressure from its people to improve the country's economy and raise living standards in a short space of time.

ECONOMY

BY ANY MEASURE, Nepal is one of the poorest, most underdeveloped countries in the world. The per capita income is only about $180 a year. This makes Nepal one of the five poorest countries in the world.

Nepal's geography, its lack of almost any natural resources and its high population growth rate make improving its economic situation very difficult.

There is a huge income distribution gap, too. About 47% of the national income goes to only 10% of the population. The poorest 40% of Nepalese earns only 10% of the national income.

Over 90% of Nepal's labor force are subsistence farmers. That means they are only able to grow enough to feed their own family, with nothing left over to sell.

In many areas of the Middle Hills, farmers cannot even do that, and food must be imported from the *terai* or other countries. To make ends meet, men in the Middle Hills are forced to migrate to the *terai* and to India to work as laborers for a few months each year. Earning minimal wages, they make just enough to get by until the next year.

In Nepal, many young men aspire to be soldiers, serving the armies of India and Great Britain. A significant source of income in the rural areas are the pensions of ex-Gurkha servicemen and the salaries active servicemen are able to send back.

A life as a career soldier is highly respected and it helps able men to escape from a life of poverty. The money they send home is often a family's only source of income.

Opposite: **A farmer plows his fields to feed his family, hoping that there may be something extra to sell in the market.**

Below: **All goods are transported through the hills on the rugged backs of porters. Development comes slowly to the interior highlands due to the lack of roads, electricity and other industrial neccesities.**

A group of Nepalese women planting rice near the town of Pokhara. Rice is the staple food of the people.

AGRICULTURE

In Nepal, agriculture depends on altitude, because changes in altitude affect the climate. Rice, for example, can only be grown up to about 6,500 feet. Corn, wheat and millet can be grown higher up, to about 9,000 feet. In the highest altitudes (up to about 14,000 feet), people depend on barley, buckwheat and potatoes.

Agriculture depends on water, too. Irrigation is usually necessary to grow rice. The higher you live, the fewer sources of water there are and the harder it is to grow rice. Below 2,100 feet, in the *terai*, it is often possible to grow two crops of rice a year.

Principle crops in Nepal are rice, wheat, corn, millet, buckwheat, barley, potatoes, sugar cane, lentils and jute. The fertile *terai* produces a sizable surplus, but Nepal still cannot feed itself and must have food aid to feed the people in the Middle Hills.

A Nepalese girl weaving carpets. The Tibetan carpet industry has become an important sector in the export economy of Nepal.

INDUSTRY

Until the mid-80s, Nepal's leading export was jute, a fiber spun from the jute plant and used mainly for burlap bags. Recently, Tibetan/Nepalese woolen carpets have become Nepal's main export and the carpet industry continues to grow rapidly. These are mainly exported to western Europe.

Nepal's leading industry, carpets, was begun by Swiss relief workers in the 1960s working with three Tibetan refugees, the only people who really knew the traditional designs and techniques. It was intended to help the thousands of refugees fleeing Communist China's takeover of Tibet.

In the mid-1980s, the carpets became very popular in Europe, particularly Germany, and the industry grew faster than anyone foresaw. Traditional designs are now being replaced by computer-generated ones, and traditional colors are replaced by more popular colors.

Almost no heavy industry exists in Nepal. Jute, sugar, cigarettes, cotton textiles, cement and leather goods are Nepal's main products. Most industrial development is in the *terai* and the valleys of Pokhara and Kathmandu. They are the only areas with adequate roads and supply of electricity.

Tourists in the Durbar Square of Kathmandu. Tourism is Nepal's biggest money earner, but many fear the effect of foreign cultures on Nepalese youth.

TOURISM

By far, Nepal's biggest industry is the service industry that has grown to cater to its tourists. About 200,000 tourists visited Nepal in 1988. Most tourists go trekking (hiking) in various areas of Nepal each year to enjoy its breathtaking scenery and the ancient culture of its people.

Tourism is often looked on as a mixed blessing for Nepal. Studies show that only about 20 cents of every dollar spent by tourists actually goes into Nepal's economy, the rest is used to import basic food and goods.

Since most cooking in Nepal is done on wood fires, thousands of trees are cut each year to cook tourists' food; trees Nepal cannot afford to lose.

Lastly, more and more Nepalese are worried about cultural pollution— young Nepalese abandoning their traditions in pursuit of Western materialism and pop culture.

TRADE

About 50% of Nepal's trade is with India. The trade balance heavily favors India and shows no signs of improving. The situation is the same overall—Nepal imports about three dollars for every dollar it is able to export.

DEVELOPMENT AID

About 40% of Nepal's annual budget comes from foreign sources in the forms of grants and low interest loans. Most of this money is designated for development projects, everything from building roads to helping farmers buy fertilizers and vaccinating children. With Nepal's lack of economy, it is likely foreign aid will be an important factor for development in the country for many more years.

Many development projects are aimed at improving social conditions. The women here are digging trenches to lay pipes for the supply of water to their village.

Many governments are giving aid. The largest donor is Japan, and other major donors include India, the United States, Australia and most of the European countries.

United Nations programs such as UNICEF (United Nations International Children's Emergency Fund), FAO (Food and Agricultural Organization), and the WHO (World Health Organization) are also active. One of Nepal's biggest donors is the World Bank and there are about 150 non-governmental organizations (NGOs) active in Nepal. NGOs are organizations such as the Red Cross and Save the Children.

NEPALESE

THERE ARE DOZENS OF DISTINCT GROUPS in Nepal. Even though all these groups have been living together for hundreds of years, there has been little blending or mixing. But there has always been a great deal of tolerance between the different groups.

In Nepal, your neighbor may worship different gods and speak a different language, but there is nothing strange about that. It is just different. Nepalese like to compare the different ways they live, and the diverse customs of various groups are a favorite topic of conversation.

Nepal is a very hierarchical society, largely influenced by the caste system which originated from Nepal's dominant religion, Hinduism, and further institutionalized by the early Malla kings of Nepal.

The hill tribes are outside the caste system, but have their own class system. Each tribe is divided into a number of clans or family groups and further sub-divided into high and low rankings.

Nepal's population can be placed into four main divisions: the Hindu caste groups, the hill tribes, the Bhotes and the Newars.

Opposite: **A beggar boy on the streets of Kathmandu. Poverty has forced many people from the hill tribes of Nepal to seek a living in the cities.**

Below: **The wrinkled lines tell the story of the difficult life in the mountains. Yet, the hill tribes remain a very friendly and hospitable people.**

Only people born of the Brahmin caste are allowed to be Hindu priests and carry out the many rites and rituals to the gods.

HINDU CASTE GROUPS

The people of the Hindu caste groups migrated to Nepal between the 12th and 15th centuries when they were pushed from their homes in India by Moslem invasions. They were originally of Aryan stock and have caucasian features, but with darker complexions. They brought their

Indo-Aryan Nepali language, which today, remains the national language of Nepal.

The Hindu religion they follow has a strict hierarchy known as the caste system. There are four groups within the caste system: Brahmins, Chhetris, Vaisyas and Sudras.

Hindus believe humans sprang from the body of Brahma, the god and creator of everything. Brahmins came from Brahma's head and mouth, Chhetris from his arms, Vaisyas from his thighs and Sudras from his feet.

A group of Chhetri children in western Nepal. These children belong to the warrior caste. Traditionally, they are not allowed to mix with children of lower castes.

At the top are the Brahmins, the priestly caste. They are forbidden by tradition to drink alcohol and eat certain foods like onions, tomatoes and eggs. A Brahmin must be called for any religious occasion and they are the only group allowed to read the Hindu religious texts.

Below the Brahmins are the Chhettris, the warrior caste. Nepal's king is a Chhetri of the Thakuri sub-caste. Traditionally, many of the Nepal's army officers are Chhetri and even today, many Chhetris join the military.

Only Brahmins and Chhetris have the right to wear the *janai*, the sacred thread draped across the chest that is the symbol of their high status.

Below the Brahmins and Chhetris are the Vaisyas, the castes of tradesman and artisans. Below them, at the bottom of the caste system, are the Sudras or occupational castes.

OCCUPATIONAL CASTES

At the lower end of the Hindu hierarchy are the occupational castes. People of these castes take their names from traditional jobs. Some examples are—Kami (blacksmiths), Damai (tailors and musicians) and Sarki (cobblers).

Today, many have abandoned their traditional occupations and work as porters and day laborers. Ready-made clothes, shoes and tools make most of their professions no longer necessary.

They are traditionally looked down on by the rest of Nepalese society and have to endure discrimination all their lives, even from the casteless hill tribes. Most people will not allow people from the occupational castes inside their homes. The occupational castes are at the bottom of the social and economic ladder in Nepal.

A hard working tailor in a village. Although vital to the community, jobs like these were considered the lowest form of work and people who did these jobs were looked down on. These attitudes are slowly changing.

A Magar woman wearing the jewelry common to the hill tribe women of Nepal. The golden nose pin is called the *phuli* (fooli).

HILL TRIBES

Nepal's many different hill tribes all crossed the high mountain passes to the north or followed the mountain trails from Burma in the east. They all have oriental features and speak their own individual languages.

The hill tribes cluster in villages at higher altitudes of about 6,000 to 9,000 feet. Young men of these tribes make up most of the famous Gurkha soldiers. Although these tribes are casteless, they are subdivided into clans of different status. Gurungs, for example, have four upper clans and 16 lower ones.

Hill tribes practice a religion that is often a combination of Buddhism and Hinduism, and sometimes, animism. In general, they are less conservative than caste Hindus and more open in their relationships. Teenage boys and girls will openly flirt and court each other, behavior that is almost never seen among their Hindu caste neighbors.

They are generally farmers who also depend on the wool and meat they can sell from the large herds of goats and sheep they keep. For at least part of the year, some members of every family must live a semi-nomadic life as they take the family's sheep and goats to high pastures at about 12,000 to 14,000 feet during the monsoon.

Young men of the Rai and Limbu tribes of eastern Nepal wear their best for a once-a-year festival. The hat they wear, the *topi*, is the national hat of Nepal.

RAIS AND LIMBUS   Also known as Kirantis, these two tribes live all through the eastern hills of Nepal extending across the border into India. The men of these tribes often carry a large *kukri*, the traditional Nepali knife with a curved blade, tucked into a long cloth wrapped around their waist.

The Kirantis are famous for the beautiful stone masonry of their farm terraces. They also build *chautara*, stone resting platforms topped by large shady pipal trees, on the trail outside villages as memorials to the dead.

TAMANGS   Tamangs are the largest of the tribal groups. They are also the most independent, retaining their own language and Buddhist religion even as other tribes fall under increasing Nepalese and Hindu influence. In Tibetan, *tamang* means "horse trader."

Tamangs live in the high hills to the north, east and west of Kathmandu. They often come to the city to work as porters and day laborers.

The preferred marriage is with your cross-cousin. For men, this is your father's sister's daughter or your mother's brother's daughter.

GURUNGS Gurungs live in the hills around Pokhara and east toward Gorkha. They (and the Magar tribe below) formed the bulk of Prithvinarayan Shah's army when he conquered the Kathmandu Valley. The military is still the main profession of Gurungs. Most families have at least one member serving in India or in the British army in Hong Kong or England.

Those remaining at home turn to farming and goat rearing. From April to September, a member of the family will take the sheep, cows and water buffaloes to high pastures even above 14,000 feet.

MAGARS Magars live in central and western Nepal, too, but generally farther south and at lower (and warmer) elevations. In the 17th century, they had a very strong kingdom in what is now Palpa, and Prithvinarayan Shah also depended heavily on them for his troops. Till today, the Magars still send the greatest number of men to the military.

As they are the southernmost of the hill tribes, they have had the longest contact with caste Hindus from India. Consequently, the Magars are the most heavily Hindu-influenced of the hill tribes.

Southern Magars have arranged marriages. The boy's parents send a representative with a bottle of rice beer to the girl's parents. If they accept the beer, the proposal is approved.

These two young Gurung teenagers take a break from carrying their load of goat and sheep skins. They will sell these skins in Kathmandu after a five-day walk from their village.

SHERPAS Saying "Sherpa" has become the equivalent of saying "mountain guide" to most tourists, but actually it should only be used for a tribe living mainly in the high valleys of the Everest region in eastern Nepal.

Born at an altitude of more than 12,000 feet at the base of the highest mountains in the world, Sherpas are naturally acclimatized to high altitude mountain climbing.

Sherpas settled in the Everest area about 300 years ago after crossing from Tibet. They were well known as traders long before their fame as mountain porters and guides.

BHOTES

All across Nepal's northern border, living in high valleys (above 9,000 feet) surrounded by Himalayan mountains are tribes of people, whose culture is essentially Tibetan called Bhotiya or Bhotes (*Bho* is another word for Tibet).

Two of the larger groups are the Thakalis and Manangis. They live in almost total isolation and each group is usually only as big as its own small valley. All of these tribes are strong Buddhists. They make their living as farmers, sheep and yak herders and traders and lately, as hoteliers. As traders, they travel all over Asia. The Manangis, for example, had received special rights for travel and trade from two previous kings of Nepal.

A group of Newar women of the farmer caste wear their distinctive costume of black *saris* with the red border along the hem.

NEWARS

Newars are the native inhabitants of the Kathmandu Valley and have been living there for over 1500 years. Their language, a mix of Tibeto-Burmese and Sanskrit origins, is one of the most complex languages in the world.

There are Newar communities in many of Nepal's larger towns, almost always working as merchants and shopkeepers. Newars built most of the temples and crafted most of the sculptures Kathmandu is famous for.

The Newars have a highly-structured caste system first imposed by the Malla kings. Newars can be either Hindu or Buddhist, or sometimes both. The caste system was used to determine your occupation by your birth: if your father was a carpenter, then that is what you will be. There is no chance of changing your job. There used to be laws detailing where you could live, what you could wear, even who you could talk to. Even today, marriages outside the caste rarely occur.

REMOTE TRIBES

There are several ethnic groups which do not fit into any category:

THARUS (see picture) are the indigenous people of the *terai*. Their natural immunity to malaria allowcd them to survive in the jungle for centuries before modern insecticides opened the *terai* for other Nepalese.

Living as marginal farmers in settlements scattered throughout the thick jungle, their shyness and lack of experience with money made them an easy mark for ruthless moneylenders, who seized the Tharus' best land when they were unable to repay their debts.

Tharus remain one of the poorest, most exploited groups in Nepal.

CHEPANGS are a tribal group living in the most remote areas of the southern–middle hills of central Nepal. Shy with outsiders they had, until recently, lived as hunter–gatherers, woodcutters and sometimes as farmers.

They were severely exploited by their better educated, more aggressive caste Hindu neighbors. The government has started several programs to try and help them.

LIFESTYLE

THERE ARE SO MANY DIFFERENT CULTURES in Nepal, the way people think and do things can vary tremendously from one house to the next. Your neighbor may speak a different language, worship different gods, even celebrate a different day for the new year. To a Nepalese, this is natural and everyone is extremely tolerant of the different customs practiced around them. A neighbor's customs are a topic of conversation, but not the cause of an argument.

Nepal is also a very structured, hierarchical society. There are divisions and rankings within your family, your extended family, your ethnic group and society as a whole. This, too, is something Nepalese are comfortable with.

The caste system has been outlawed by the government, but still plays a large role in everyday life. Attitudes are slowly changing, particularly in urban areas, and low caste people may not carry the stigma they once did. The government is trying to widen opportunities for everyone.

Names in Nepal are traditionally much more than simply a name. Names indicate your caste or group, your profession, and perhaps, even where you come from.

If you met Mr. Khatiwanda, you will know from his name that he is a Brahmin and probably from western Nepal. Mr. Pokhrel is a Brahmin, too, but from the east. Mr. Sakya is a Newar, and works as a silver or goldsmith. As interaction between castes is forbidden, knowing a person's name also settles the question of whether you can accept the rice they cooked or visit each other's homes. This is no longer as true as it once was.

Opposite: **An infant is being bathed in cold water. The use of hot water for bathing is almost unknown in the hills where fuel wood is precious.**

Below: **Leaves and plants are woven tightly together to form a water-proof roof. The leaves will also trap the heat to keep the house warm on cold nights.**

It is common to find extended families of different generations living together in a single household. The extended family is made up of uncles, aunts and cousins.

FAMILY STRUCTURE

When a Nepalese says "my family," he or she is speaking of a much larger immediate family than Americans usually have. Cousins are called brothers and sisters, a mother's oldest sister is called oldest-mother, a father's youngest brother is youngest-father and so on.

Several generations commonly live in a single household. Sons customarily stay in the home even after marriage, bringing their new wife with them.

All the money earned goes into a family treasury that is controlled by the head of the household, usually the oldest male. He has the final say in all important family decisions. This can include which children will study in school, what jobs they can do, and whom they will marry.

Women in Bhote cultures have a stronger position at home and can be very assertive. Their men are away trading most of the time, so the women take over much of the decision-making.

GROWING UP

Name-giving is the first important milestone for the infant in many Hindu homes. Customs vary from group to group, but the name is determined by an astrologer based on the exact time of birth.

Almost all groups have a rice-feeding ceremony when a baby is about six months old, called *pausni* in Nepali. Many guests are invited for this and the parents will give a big feast. Guests often give the infant money to wish for its future prosperity.

During a Newar *pausni*, several objects may be placed in front of the baby—dirt, unhusked rice, a brick, toys, a pen, or a book. The parents and priest predict the child's future talents or occupation based on which object the infant reaches for first.

At the age of about five, male Brahmins and Chhetris have their head shaved except for a small tuft of hair toward the back of the head called a *tupi*. The *tupi* indicates that the boy is a Hindu.

Although many Nepalese are poor, they love children and spoil them terribly.

PUBERTY

When approaching puberty, male Brahmins and Chhetris receive a *janai*, a sacred thread (actually three loops of cotton twine), worn over the right shoulder and under the left arm. The *janai* is a sign of his high caste and is changed once a year, on the full moon of July or August. After completing this ceremony, he can eat with the adult men for the first time.

At the age of 12, Buddhist Newar boys have their heads shaved, are bathed, dressed in saffron robes, given alms bowls and sent off begging, as the Buddha did thousands of years ago. They are only sent to their relative's and neighbor's houses and return home on the same day.

Before they reach puberty, Newar girls go through their first marriage—to a *bel* fruit (wood apple)! The *bel* represents the god Subarna Kumar.

Newar boys celebrate the onset of puberty with the *Bratabhanda* ceremony. For today, the boys will follow the footsteps of the Buddha and go begging from house to house .

Since the full marriage rites can only be given once, the girl's subsequent marriage is of secondary importance and she is free to divorce and marry again, or re-marry if she becomes a widow.

In Hindu and Newar homes, a daughter's puberty is no cause for celebration. During her first menstruation, she is taken and locked in a room for 14 days. Considered unclean, she is forbidden to see or be seen by the men of the house or to touch any food but her own. Sometimes, even the women of her own house may avoid her touch.

MARRIAGE

Almost all marriages are between members of the same caste or ethnic groups. Inter-caste marriages are extremely rare, as both husband and wife will be cut off from their respective families.

The marriages of caste Hindus and the Newars are usually arranged by the parents. A relative of one side acts as a go-between, relaying photos of the boy and girl and conducting the necessary convincing and negotiations. Sometimes the couple is allowed to meet, but only if accompanied by plenty of chaperones.

The hill tribes have three types of marriages. There are arranged marriages, or the boy and girl may court and choose each other, or the boy may capture/kidnap the girl. He then has three days to convince her and after that must release her if she still refuses. Actual wedding customs, though, vary widely from group to group.

Although it is illegal, polygamy still occurs in Nepal. The most common reason for marrying another woman is because the wife is unable to bear a son. All the wives may live in the same household, or separately.

Bhotes, because their men are gone for long periods on trading trips, practice polyandry and a woman may marry several brothers at the same time. All children are considered the oldest brother's.

A Hindu wedding in Nepal. The bride sits with her head covered while Brahmin priests pray for the gods' blessing.

DOMESTIC ARCHITECTURE

Houses in Nepal vary according to the people who live in them and the climates they are built in. Many people in the *terai* build their homes on stilts and keep their animals below. Living higher is some protection from the snakes, animals and mosquitoes. It is also much cooler and breezier off the ground. Each house stands in its own compound.

Higher up in the hills, where there are fewer snakes and winters are colder, the houses are more solid, with thick stone walls and thatched or slate tile roofs. Windows are small, without glass panes. There is no chimney for the fire, either. The creosote from the fire coats the wood above and protects it from bugs. Houses are closer together and two or three homes may share a compound.

In the high Himalayan region, people live on the second floor like in the *terai,* but it is to get away from the cold. That is also the reason why homes share a common wall with their neighbor; there is less chance for the cold to get in. Animals live beneath the house and their body heat helps to warm the rooms above. The houses are constructed of stone and wood, with wooden shingles weighed down by heavy stones.

THE HEARTH

Each ethnic group places special importance on the hearth and cooking area.

A non-Brahmin should never enter the cooking area in a Brahmin house. To do so would pollute the area and a religious "cleansing" ceremony must be performed. A Brahmin male will take off his clothes and wrap a length of white cloth called a *dhoti* around himself before he steps into the hearth area to eat.

In the Middle Hills and Himalayas, though, a guest will immediately be given the best seat by the hearth—on the right side near the back wall of the hearth.

Most social activity takes place around the fire, which is in an open pit with an iron tripod to put pots on. People here, too, respect the hearth and are careful not to throw anything which could be considered "dirty" into it.

In the northern hills, the hearth is the center of the house. Guests are asked to sit by the fire as soon as they come in.

In the villages, many house chores take place outside the house. It is common to do the washing at the nearest spring or river.

A TYPICAL DAY IN THE VILLAGE

Work in the village begins before the roosters crow. There is wood to be gathered, fodder to be cut and water to be fetched. Water may come from a nearby well or from a stream or tap over an hour's walk away. As the forests disappear, water is disappearing too, and people have to walk farther and farther for both.

The fire is lit and cooking starts as soon as the household stirs. There may be tea and sugar to drink, but probably not for every morning. Most people eat *derdho*—a mix of millet, corn and wheat flour boiled into a thick paste. To go with this, there may be lentil soup and some vegetable curry (potato is most common) or just vegetables with broth. If the family cow or water buffalo has a calf, there may be milk or yogurt.

After eating, some children go off to school, others help out in the fields or at home. School starts at 10 a.m.

Farm work, grazing cattle, getting wood or water, everything is done by hand and carried on the back. After school, children may play or join their parents at work.

People use the sun, not watches, to tell time. As the sun begins to set, everyone gathers around the fire. Light may come from a tiny kerosene lamp or just from the fire. After eating (probably *derdho* again), the family gathers to talk until everyone has gone to sleep.

A TYPICAL DAY IN TOWN

People rise early in town, too. Nothing tastes better than a steaming glass of Nepalese milk tea on a cold morning. Water may be in the house or from a nearby tap. Mother starts work right away because it takes about two hours to cook on her single kerosene stove. She prepares a meal of rice, lentil soup, vegetable curry, maybe milk, yogurt, or meat. Children get ready for school or play.

Father then goes to his shop or office, and mother begins her housework. If parents can, they send their children to private English language schools. School buses may be anything from a rickshaw to a rickety old van packed with classmates.

Mother washes the dishes and clothes at the nearest communal tap and then goes to market to buy the day's vegetables and food. There is no refrigerator to store a week's groceries. After school, children play, study, or maybe go see the new Indian movie in town—the cheap seats are only about 5 cents.

Father finishes his work at 5 p.m. and makes his way home slowly. He talks to friends, maybe over a cup of tea or local liquor, stops at the newsstand to browse through the latest books and magazines. When he comes home, he checks his children's studies. In each room candles are always handy, in case there is another blackout.

The evening meal is late, 8 p.m. or after, and everyone goes to bed soon afterward.

The ride home in a bicycle rickshaw may take longer, but these school children happily look forward to playing with their friends at home.

WOMEN IN NEPAL

Opposite: **In the cities, some girls from middle income families are sent to English language schools. But after completing their studies, they are still expected to marry and be traditional housewifes.**

Above: **Nepalese women are also an unseen economic force. Many cottage industries, such as spinning and weaving, are carried out by them.**

Surveys have shown that women in the village do over 70% of the work. This includes fetching water, fodder and firewood, hoeing, weeding, harvesting, every kind of work. There are only the most basic tools and everything is done by hand, everything is carried on someone's back.

A new bride usually lives with her husband's family and must earn the respect of her in-laws through hard work. Though life is not always rosy, divorce is almost unheard of.

Women have almost no decision-making power. Women in caste Hindu homes, in particular, are powerless. Women in Bhote families may be very powerful because the men are away on trading trips so much of the time. Women in the hill tribes are somewhere in-between.

Sons are hoped for, daughters are necessary to do field work. Because the expenses during marriage must be paid by her family, girls are considered a burden as well as a source of labor. Sons are sent to school, girls are sent to work. Only 18% of Nepalese women can read and write.

The Nepalese government is trying to improve the condition of women, but women are still under-represented and discriminated against in many areas of Nepalese life.

A baby is inoculated against diseases. There is always a long line at these free health clinics and mothers must sometimes walk for days to reach one.

HEALTH CARE

One out of 10 children in Nepal die before the age of one. Three out of 20 do not survive beyond the age of five. One reason why families want many children is because they believe some will inevitably die.

Many of the health problems come from poor hygiene and sanitation. Few houses have toilets. People use the nearby fields or streams and then clean themselves with water using the left hand. Worms and diarrheal diseases are easily spread in this way. Thirty-three percent of child deaths are caused by diarrhea.

The government is trying to provide a hospital in every district and a healthpost in every *panchayat*. Still, it will take hours for people to travel to the healthpost and days to reach the hospital. And once they arrive there, the doctor or medicine may not be available due to transportation and communication problems.

Many people still go to a traditional faith healer, called a *jankri,* if they are sick. The *jankri* supposedly removes the cause of the illness, often by going into a trance while beating on a drum. Some *jankri* do have a great deal of real knowledge about medicinal plants and they mix herbal medicines to treat illnesses.

EDUCATION

Going to school in rural Nepal is a totally different experience. Students all walk to school and this may take two hours. Lessons are usually conducted outdoors with around 40 students to a class. Classrooms are used only when necessary as they are dark and cold due to the lack of electricity. Few or no textbooks are available, so most students are taught to memorize their lessons.

Nepal's literacy rate today is 34%. Considering that in the 1950s the literacy rate was only 5%, Nepal has come a long way despite the difficulties of providing enough teachers and textbooks.

A typical mud-bricked schoolhouse. Before lessons, the students and teachers gather to sing the national anthem and do some exercises.

The preparation of a funeral pyre takes place at Pashupatinath, the most sacred temple in Nepal. Hindus believe in cremating their dead and then scattering the ashes into a river.

DEATH

Death is treated in different ways in different cultures. Hindus carry their dead to the bank of the nearest river and cremate the body. They pick out a small piece of bone and throw the ashes in the river. They believe that the ashes will eventually reach the sacred waters of the Ganges in India.

The hill tribes of Magars and Tamangs cremate their dead, but on top of a hill, not by a river. Gurungs either cremate or bury their dead. A priest decides which, based on the position of the stars at the time of death.

All the hill tribes have elaborate ceremonies to mark the first anniversary of death. During this ceremony, the family of the dead person will have to give a large feast for the entire village.

In the Himalayan region, wood is scarce and so cremation is difficult. Often, the land is also too rocky for digging graves. The Bhotes, who live in this area, take the body to a high place, chop it into little pieces, and leave it for the birds to eat.

COMMON COURTESIES AND ETIQUETTE

When Nepalese meet each other or leave each other, they join their hands in front of them in a prayer-like gesture and say *namaste* or sometimes *namaskar*. These are from Sanskrit words which mean "I bow to the god in you."

Himalayan people drape a thin white scarf called a *khata* around the neck of someone they want to show respect to or someone leaving on a trip.

Nepalese seldom say *dhanyabad* (thank you). Nor do people open a present when it is given. To avoid any chance of embarrassing anyone, they open it in private.

The feet are the dirtiest part of the body, the head the most sacred. A Nepalese will never step over a person. If a Nepalese touches you with his feet by accident, he will immediately reach down, touch your feet and then touch his own head as if to say, "I am sorry. Your feet are higher than my head."

Always give and take with the right hand. Since the left hand is used to clean yourself after using the toilet, it is considered very dirty.

RELIGION

NEPAL'S POPULATION is about 90% Hindu, 8% Buddhist and 2% Moslem according to the last census. In everyday life, though, the line between Hindu and Buddhist is far from clear. Many people follow both religions. Hinduism, in particular, is a part of everyday life as it is integrated into daily routines such as shopping or going to work.

Because the Buddha is considered a form of the Hindu god, Vishnu, Buddha's teachings are well-known and have a great influence even among Nepalese Hindus.

Opposite: **This Buddhist** *gomba,* **or monastery, was built 500 years ago.**

Below: **A Brahmin priest gives a** *tika* **to a young girl. The** *tika* **is a sign of blessing and a symbol of knowledge.**

Opposite: **A centuries-old sculpture of the Hindu god Vishnu. He is known as the Preserver of the Universe.**

HINDUISM

Hinduism, the oldest living faith in the world, has no person who can be identified as its founder. There is no governing, regulating body, and there is no specific dogma that can be pointed at to say, "this is what a Hindu believes."

The vast body of philosophy from which Hindus define their beliefs is called the *Vedas*, 1,008 hymns and revelations of saints and seers first recorded well over 1,000 years ago.

Hinduism encompasses many beliefs, so many that one may directly contradict another. In Hindu philosophy, there are more than one righteous path to understanding the mysteries of life. It is up to the individual's own capacities, attitudes and requirements to build his or her own system of beliefs.

Hindus believe that after death, they are reborn, moving up or down a universal ladder. Their actions now determine their next life. If they are bad, they may be reborn as a lower caste or as animals or even as insects.

If they do great good in this life, earning much *dharma* or merit, then their next life will be enriched. After thousands of lives they may be able to climb into heaven, released from the cycle of life and death at last.

Their condition in this world and the random things that happen in their lives, are their *karma* or destiny. It does no good to feel anger and rebel against *karma*. *Karma* is accepted and borne. This attitude of tolerance helps the Nepalese bear their poverty, but it may make motivation for change difficult.

HINDU GODS

One Hindu text states that there are 300 million gods, and Hindus themselves actively worship hundreds. But only three stand out: Bhrama the Creator, Vishnu the Preserver and Shiva the Destroyer. These three gods combine to become Bhraman, the ultimate divinity found in everything.

The same god may be called a dozen different names and manifest themselves in several different forms. Vishnu, for example, has 10 different forms, including a lion, a dwarf, the Hindu hero Krishna, and even the Buddha. The Nepalese consider the king himself to be a manifestation of Vishnu.

Shiva, with over 108 different names, is the god most worshiped in Nepal. Known as the destroyer, he is also called the "bright or happy one," and is honored as Lord of the Dance. He is often pictured as an ascetic, body smeared with ashes and wrapped in leopard skin, wandering the far corners or meditating at his home on Mount Kailash in Tibet. It is believed that the waters of the Ganges River springs from the mat of hair piled high on his head.

Ganesh, Shiva's son, is one of everybody's favorite gods. His father cut off his head by mistake and to appease his wife, swore to replace it with the first living thing he found—an elephant. With his elephant head and roly-poly body, Ganesh does not look like a typical immortal. Still, he is the god most people would first turn to for their requests.

Durga is one of the forms that Shiva's wife, Parbati. Durga is the goddess worshiped during the festival of Dasain for her victory over an evil demon.

Laxmi, the goddess of wealth, is appealed to during the festival of Tihar.

Saraswati, the goddess of wisdom, is usually shown riding a swan and playing a sitar.

Indra the god of rain is prayed to during the monsoons.

BUDDHISM

The Buddha's real name is Siddhartha Gautama. Buddha (an honorary title meaning the "enlightened one") was born around 623 B.C. in Lumbini, which is now part of Nepal's *terai*. Born into a rich, perhaps noble family, he led a sheltered life of luxury and ease in several palaces.

Being curious about life outside, he made several secret trips outside the palace. Shocked by the pain, death and suffering of the people, he decided to renounce everything, even his wife and son, to try and understand what he had seen.

For the next six years, he went through every form of deprivation as he meditated and searched for the answers to life. Finally realizing them, he became the Buddha. For the rest of his life he walked with a group of disciples, talking with anyone who listened or asked and spreading his message. He died at Bodh Ghaya in India.

White prayer flags are hung outside temples and monasteries as the people believe the winds will carry their prayers to heaven.

All Buddhists believe that life is a cycle of birth, death and rebirth in a wheel of life. Your rebirth is based on your *karma*, which is the sum result of your actions, words and thoughts in life. A Buddhist's goal is to break the cycle of rebirth by living a life of self-detachment and deprivation. If a Buddhist does this, he or she attains *nirvana* (release from life).

Several Buddhist schools have evolved since the Buddha's life thousands of years ago. The Theravada school is followed in Sri Lanka

THE TEACHINGS OF BUDDHA

Today, in Lumbini, there is a small temple on the spot where Buddha was supposedly born, but little else to commemorate him. Brick ruins of monasteries which were built 1,000 years ago stand in the tall grass and there is a mound and pillar built in 250 B.C. by Ashok, the great Indian emperor. The Buddha's teachings, though, remain and have spread throughout Asia to Japan, Indo-China and even to the ancient kingdoms of Indonesia.

THE FOUR NOBLE TRUTHS
—In all our lives there is pain from disease, suffering, birth and death.
—The basic cause of these lie in our desires for material things, for pleasures and for people.
—Detachment from these desires ends pain and gives an escape from the cycle of rebirth.
—The eightfold path is the way to attain this detachment.

THE EIGHTFOLD PATH
Right understanding, right thought, right speech, right action, right livelihood, right effort, right mindfulness and right concentration.

Buddhist monks chanting. Although the religion traveled from Nepal to Tibet, rites and forms of worship now draw inspiration from the latter.

and Southeast Asia. The Mahayana school has influenced Tibet, Nepal and north Asia.

One important difference in Theravada philosophy is that you are only concerned with your own release from the cycle. The Mahayana says that if you find the way yourself, you must "go back" and try and help others do the same.

71

A woman spins a prayer wheel. These objects help those who are unable to read or recite the Pali scriptures of Buddhism.

IN DAILY LIFE

Each morning in Nepal the streets are full of people going to the neighborhood shrine for *puja* (worship). Each carries a tray with colored powder, flower petals, some grains of rice, a few small sweets, and a small bell. All this will be used in worship at the temple.

Many people you meet in the morning will have flower petals in their hair. This is part of *prasad,* the blessing received from the gods in return for worshiping them. The mark many people wear on their forehead, the *tika*, is another sign of blessing, symbolic of the third eye of inner wisdom and vision.

They believe divinity is in everything, in themselves, in the plants and animals and even in the rocks. Roads are built around large rocks and trees rather than removing them and disturbing their divinity. It is impossible for the Nepalese to separate their daily lives from religion as what they do and say affects them in this life and the next.

Hindus worship the cow as their Divine Mother, and also as a symbol of fertility. The cow's products and by-products, milk and yogurt, even dung and urine, have special religious significance. A Hindu would never think of killing a cow or eating beef. Cows wander loose everywhere. They have good reason to feel secure: the penalty for killing a cow even by accident can be up to 20 years in jail!

73

Both father and son are Moslems. They can be recognized by the skullcaps on their heads which are of Middle Eastern origin.

OTHER RELIGIONS

About 2% of Nepal's population is Islamic. Almost all Moslems live in the *terai*. In some places they are in the majority. There is a very small Christian population. In certain remote corners of the Himalayan area, Bon, the Tibetan religion before Buddhism is still followed.

In the face of cultural and religious diversity, the Nepalese exercise great tolerance and mutual respect for the beliefs of others. They are proud of the fact that there has never been any religious conflict in the history of Nepal.

FOLK BELIEFS

There are customs, superstitions and rituals, both large and small, to cover almost all aspects of everyday life. Because of Nepal's cultural diversity, customs which are important or offensive to one culture may be nothing to another. Here are some customs and beliefs:

Never blow out a light with your breath; wave something, even just your hand, to fan out the flame.

After lighting a lamp or just switching on an electric light for the first time that day, a Nepalese will make a *namaste* gesture toward the light.

Fresh water should be fetched every morning; water that stands overnight is no longer clean.

Before serving food, a small bit of rice will be placed in the fire as an offering to the gods.

When you see a baby for the first time, give some money (a rupee or a few coins) to guarantee its future prosperity.

If a bee hovers near you, good fortune is coming, too.

The Nepalese travel often, and there are a whole set of beliefs about travel:

If your feet itch, you will be traveling soon.

Some people take a betel nut, a coin, and some rice wrapped in a cloth to ensure a safe trip.

It is unlucky to start a trip on a Tuesday.

It is unlucky to leave under a new moon.

A large jug full of water on both sides of the doorway ensures a safe trip.

Try not to come back on Saturday.

Mothers threaten their naughty children with, "the foreigner will come and eat you!" Nepalese had enough strange creatures and spirits even before foreigner started arriving:

A *jhumi* will grab you and lead you away from your house without your knowledge if you leave early in the morning without telling anyone.

If you meet a beautiful young woman late at night, look at her feet. If they're pointed backwards, run! She's a *kichkanni*, the spirit of a dead woman.

A *murkatta*, a dead man's spirit, wanders around headless.

If you wake up, but don't feel you can get up, it's a *khya* holding you down. If a *khya* gets upset, it tickles you to death.

Pret and *pishach*, unhappy spirits, wait at crossroads and cremation sites to chase people and make them sick.

LANGUAGE

THERE ARE OVER A DOZEN LANGUAGES spoken in Nepal and each language has many different dialects. In fact, dialects change with almost every ridge you cross. For example, a Tamang from Dhading in central Nepal will have a hard time understanding a Tamang from Taplejung in the east. This is Nepal's geography at work again.

Nepali is the national language and the one people from different groups use with each other. Nepali is an Indo-European language and has many similarities to the Hindi language of northern India. They use the same script and have many similarities in grammar and vocabulary.

THE NEPALI LANGUAGE

Nepali sentence structure is very different from English. The usual order is subject-object-verb. There are "markers" to identify the words which are the subject, object or indirect object. The marker for the subject is *le*, for indirect object the marker is *laai*. For example:

> Ram<u>le</u> Sita<u>laai</u> paani diyo.
> Ram to Sita water gave.
> (Ram gave water to Sita.)

There are two different verbs that share the function of the English verb "to be." Roughly, one form is used when describing something (at that moment) while the other is used for permanent state of beings.

Nepali also has some sounds that English does not have. For example, there are two "d" sounds, while English has only one. Nepali also has several aspirated sounds—like an extra "h" to a sound. This is very difficult to hear and pick up. For example, "ka" and "kha."

Opposite: **Scriptures are inscribed by a mountain pass to praise God and to protect all those who travel on this precarious path.**

LANGUAGE AS ETIQUETTE

The Nepali language can be very formal and polite. Even the words you use will change according to whether you are talking to a friend, a shopkeeper, your parents or a high official. There is even a separate vocabulary used only when speaking to the royal family.

The words you use when talking to someone depends on their status relative to you. You use higher words with people you should show respect to and lower words with people who should show you respect. That means a child talking to his parents will use one vocabulary to ask them a question, but the parents will use another form to answer the children.

It is the same at work. Your boss will use words and forms that definitely lets you know that he or she is the boss. But with his or her own boss, he or she will use other words that show respect to the superior.

For many people in Nepal, books are a luxury as they may be illiterate or just too poor to afford them.

WRITING

The Devanagri script is very old. It is the same script used to write Hindi. Each of the characters represents a sound, not a letter. Words are formed by joining the characters with a line across the top. The Nepalese write below the line on lined paper.

Nepal is a nation of linguists. It is not uncommon for even young children to speak two or three different languages. Most children will start out speaking their own group's language in the home, then learn Nepali in the school. They will usually pick up Hindi as they grow up. In school, they will also study English.

THE DIFFERENT PERSONS IN YOU

There are many different ways to say "you," depending on the respect you should give, or want to give, the person you are talking to:

yaahaa — Very polite.

hajur — Polite, often used by women when talking to their husband.

tapaai — The most common form used in everyday conversation with casual friends or shopkeepers.

timi — Used with good friends, children, or lower caste people, sometimes used by a husband with his wife. It can imply affection, or a sense of superiority, or both.

ta — Used with animals, young children, people of very low status, or someone you want to fight with. It can imply great affection, or a total lack of respect.

OTHER LANGUAGES

The languages of the hill tribes and Bhotes are called Tibeto-Burmese languages. They are a little like Chinese and are monosyllabic and tonal. To speak correctly, you must give a word the right stress and tone, either rising or falling. The same syllable may have several meanings based on the different stresses you use as you say it.

The Bhote languages in particular are very close to Tibetan and use Tibetan script when writing.

Newari, the language of the Newars, is an Indo-European language that has absorbed a great deal of influence from Tibeto-Burmese. It is one of the most difficult languages in the world to learn.

In the *terai,* there are a great number of Indo-European languages spoken. The two most widely spoken languages after Nepali are Bhojpuri and Maithili. These are very different from Nepali. Although they both have common roots, a Nepali speaker and a Maithili speaker will have a very hard time understanding each other.

NEPALESE PROVERBS

What's something totally insignificant? It is, "a cumin seed on an elephant's trunk." The Nepalese have all kinds of proverbs and sayings, which reflect the world they live in. Some of them are easy for us to understand, some require a little reflection:

> He can't face a live tiger, but he'll pull the whiskers off a dead one.
> He couldn't see a buffalo on himself, but he finds a louse on someone else.
> Too many cats kill no mice.
> If you need a drink, you have to find a spring.
> Give someone a drink, but don't show them the spring.
> No one sits by a burnt-out fire.
> A knot tied with a laugh is untied with tears.
> Dress according to the land you are in.
> It takes a hundred more lies to hide the first.
> The sun can't be covered by your hand.
> The carpenter's staircase is broken.

ARTS

IN KATHMANDU IT IS EASY TO WALK PAST a 1000-year-old statue without even knowing it. As daily life swirls around, masterpieces in wood, stone, metal and brick are treated with the casualness of an old friend. Sometimes it is hard for us, used to hushed pristine museums, to understand. Great works of art are as much a part of daily life and routine as the morning cup of tea. To Nepalese, their art is not to be locked away and viewed from a distance on special occasions; it is an ingredient in their daily environment, to be touched, sat on, worshiped, or even used to entertain little children.

Nepal's greatest fine arts are in the forms of sculpture and architecture. There is almost no secular art at all. Almost all Nepalese art is generated for worshiping the two great religious traditions that shape so much of life in the country: Hinduism and Buddhism.

And Nepalese art is mostly anonymous. We know the names of the patrons, but not the names of the artists and craftsmen who executed their commissions.

Not so with music. By far the favorite subject is romance, and songwriters are household names. Children are brought up to sing and dance without embarrassment, and when they get older their ability to sing with wit and dance with grace can help them win the heart of that special someone. In a country largely free of television and radio, Nepalese still rely on each other for entertainment.

MUSIC

The Nepalese love music. Walk through any village and you are bound to hear someone singing, or the lilting sound of a flute, or the catchy rhythm of a drum. Radios are becoming more common but still, in most places in Nepal, if you want to hear music, you make it yourself.

A wedding would not be possible in Nepal without a band to go ahead announcing the approach of a wedding party. In the far west, the band is mostly drums. In the Middle Hills, people blow the *shanai*, an oboe-like instrument, and big horns that curve back and over. In the cities, bands with Western instruments blast out Western and Hindi pop songs in a style that is half-polka, half-Dixieland and all fun.

The hymns and religious songs sung at temples are accompanied by drums, large cymbals and tiny finger ones, flutes and harmoniums. In Buddhist monasteries high in the Himals, lamas on rooftops play huge horns that are 10 to 15 feet long. Their low bass rumble echoes through the high mountain valleys and can be heard for miles.

SONG

Singing is almost a national sport in Nepal. At many festivals in the Middle Hills, a singing competition is always one of the main attractions.

There are two teams, boys and girls. One side sings a short verse, asking a rhetoric question, criticizing the other side's song or dress, or telling a story. As the one side sings, the other side must think up a reply, wittier and more poetic. Onlookers offer judgments. Highest marks go for the wit of the verses. The sides may go back and forth all night, ending with an agreement to meet at the same place, same time next year.

One of the great traditions of Nepalese music, and one that is fast disappearing, is the *gaini*. *Gaini* are wandering minstrels that go from town to town and literally sing for their supper. They sing of famous old stories and the latest rumors and gossip. They live on the donations from the crowd of villagers who gather to listen. Once, a whole family used to travel together, the son learning the songs at his father's knee. These days, *gaini* are slowly fading away in the age of radios and walkmans.

There are nationwide competitions every year for folk songs. The wit and poetry of the verses are at least as important as the melody and singer's voice.

DRAMA

Traditional dramas retell the great adventures of the *Ramayana* and *Mahabharata*. These are performed during religious festivals and sponsored by neighborhood religious organizations.

There is also a modern, young drama movement. These are mainly social dramas about the new problems confronting Nepal's increasingly urban, Western-influenced population: youthful alienation, evil schemers, drugs, and even topics such as the position of women in society and corruption.

Comedy has a long tradition in Nepal and no drama would be complete without a comic interlude or two, sometimes even three! In recent years, comic reviews have toured the larger towns and been a big success.

The biggest comic event of the year occurs during the Gai Jatra festival. Held at the Royal Academy in Kathmandu, it is the one day of the year when you can poke fun at anything or anybody, no matter how big or powerful they are. The are no rules; anything can be said and no one can take offense. The results are uproarious and cassettes of the evening are always bestsellers.

DANCE

Religious dances are very common in Nepal. The dancers wear elaborate costumes and huge masks and headdresses. Their dances depict the struggles and triumphs of the gods over demons. An example are the dancers of the Indra Jatra festival, who walk through the streets and dance at the temples and the old palace.

Buddhists have a strong tradition of religious dance, too. Twice a year, in the Mount Everest area, the Sherpas hold a three-day epic dance re-enacting the triumph of Buddhism over the old Bon religion. People from all over the world come to see the elaborate costumes, masks and the controlled energy of the dancers.

Almost every ethnic group has its own folk dance style. Himalayan people put their arms around each other's shoulders and form a sort of chorus line. Rai and Limbus hold hands (men and women) and dance slowly in a circle.

In caste Hindu culture, men and women rarely dance together, and women rarely dance at all. Traditionally, one or two men will dance surrounded by a close circle of people singing, clapping and urging the swirling dancers on.

In this Gurung village, two young girls dance the story of a long deceased king and queen. Sadly, with the influence of pop culture, many young people are turning away from local traditions.

These Brahmin priests are singing and reciting verses from a religious song they have published. They will try to sell these to the crowds who have gathered to hear them.

LITERATURE

Nepal is also a nation of poets. There are a number of poetry competitions throughout the year. These are often broadcast over the radio and, with the start of television in some areas in the late 1980s, the finals are shown on the screen as well.

The birthdays of the most famous poets are celebrated with parades and recitations of their poems. Prasad Devkota, who lived from 1909 to 1959 is considered one of Nepal's greatest poets. The royal family also writes poetry. Several of the queen's poems have become popular songs.

Brahmins, members of the religious caste, sometimes privately publish a booklet of long poems they have written. They recite the poem in public, singing it to a simple melody and sell the booklets to the audience who has gathered to hear them. These poems are religious homilies, using a story to make a point from Hindu sciptures.

THE *MAHABHRATA* AND THE *RAMAYANA*

The Hindu epics combine the teachings of the *Vedas* with great stories and legends. They have been entertaining and teaching children and adults alike for thousands of years. Children can still recount the adventures of their favorite heroes.

Like the Greek *Iliad* the stories have a basis in history, with the gods and goddesses playing an active role in the affairs of man. The *Mahabharata* recounts the heroic struggle of five brothers, the Pandava, against their five evil cousins. Within the *Mahabhrata*, the *Bhagavad Gita* (Song of God), presents the essence of Hinduism.

The *Ramayana* centers on the adventures of the great hero Ram, his wife Sita, and his brother Laxman. Sita is kidnapped by the terrible demon Ravenna. After much searching, Ram's friend, the monkey king Hanuman, finds her on the island of Sri Lanka. Following a terrific battle, Ram finally kills the demon and rescues Sita with Hanuman's help.

Nepal figures in both epics. The great Nepalese king, Yalambar, is killed in the *Mahabhrata's* climactic battle. In the *Ramayana*, Ram wins the hands of Sita in a competition in Sita's home, Janakpur, in Nepal's *terai*.

The Buddhist "wheel of life" is painted in the Tibetan style and is called a *thangka*.

PAINTING

There are two main painting traditions in Nepal, one with its roots in the south, the other in the north. Paintings, too, are mainly devoted to religious themes.

In the south are examples of Newari paintings from the 11th century. These are miniatures to illustrate manuscripts, and the style is derived from Indian work. By the 15th century, Brahminical manuscripts were being beautifully decorated by miniatures similar to an Indian style called *Pahari*. These painters were all Chitrakars, the painter's caste in the rigid caste system used by the Malla kings.

From the 14th century, Nepalese painters started to work on scrolls inspired by Tibetan scroll paintings called *thangka*. *Thangka* are religious paintings of Buddha and other Buddhists themes such as "the wheel of life." Nepalese artists traveled to Tibet and across Central Asia and brought this new art form back to Nepal.

Today, Tibetan *thangka*-style paintings are becoming well known and popular in the West. Rich in color, elaborate in design and extremely detailed, their appeal is easy to see. Newari paintings, called *paubha* or *pati,* documents all aspects of religious life. They are still done, but for the most part have not caught on in the profitable tourist market.

SCULPTURE

The greatest period of sculpture came under the Malla kings from the 15th to 17th centuries. Most sculpture was made to decorate the palaces and temples and shaped by Newar craftsmanship. Sculpturing was not considered a very respectable profession. The people who did these beautiful statues were not considered worthy of noting and so we do not know the names of any of these master artists.

Sculptors worked with wood, stone and metal (usually brass). There are stone sculptures from as long ago as the 6th century and the wooden sculptures on some of the temples are more than 900 years old.

Nepalese sculptors liked to work in metal best of all. They used the lost wax method: making a wax model to make a clay mold, both of which are destroyed when the statue is actually made. Another popular technique was *repousse*. This means using a hammer and chisel to tap and pound a design into a sheet of metal, usually copper.

Both of these methods are still being used today. If you walk down the streets of Patan, you will still hear the clinking sound of hammers tapping on metal.

Craftsmen still work in the traditional manner. A large share of the work is aimed at the tourist market.

ORIGINS OF THE PAGODA

At the end of the 13th century, a master Nepalese architect, known today as Arniko, traveled north at the invitation of the Tibetans. As he and his team of 24 assistants completed several projects, Arniko's reputation spread and he came to the attention of the Ming emperor of China. Arniko joined the court of the emperor and today, one of his buildings stands in Beijing. The pagoda-style seen today all through East Asia owes its origins to this remarkable and little-known man.

ARCHITECTURE

Religious architecture is Nepal's main contribution to world art. Seven places in the Kathmandu Valley have been designated by UNESCO as world heritage landmarks. No place in the world has so many important landmarks in such a small area.

Much of Nepal's architecture is the work of Newar craftsmen working during the time of the Malla kings, particularly from the 15th through the 17th century. Builders and craftsmen were paid from the state treasuries, and no expense was spared. They built with brick, wood and stone. Today, the palace squares remain much as they were centuries ago.

Most of these architectural treasures can still be marveled at in the Durbar squares of Bhaktapur, Kathmandu and Patan. These squares contain the royal palaces of the old kingdoms.

The same cannot be said for the old neighborhoods of the valley. The old brick and tile buildings are being rapidly replaced by concrete and corrugated tin.

In the 19th and 20th centuries, the Rana prime ministers filled Kathmandu with huge European-style palaces. Today, the largest of their palaces are government offices and hotels.

All over Buddhist areas of Nepal you will find structures that are half-sculpture, half-architecture called *stupas*. Two of the largest and most beautiful are at Boudhanath and Swayambhu in the Kathmandu Valley.

Stupas are Buddhist representations of the universe. The mound represents earth, water, air and fire.

The eyes are those of the Buddha, the third eye is the eye of true knowledge, the nose is the number one and represents unity.

The 13 rings of the spire are the 13 degrees of knowledge, and the ladder to *nirvana* is represented by an umbrella-like structure at the top.

LEISURE

LIFE IN NEPAL moves at a slower pace than it does in the United States. There are no shopping malls and most stores are only a single small room, often no bigger than a closet. There are none of the luxury goods, so taken for granted in the United States, to put in the stores anyway.

Television affects only a small portion of the population in Kathmandu and the *terai,* and only broadcasts for a few hours a day. There is only one radio station, and it broadcasts for only part of the day. There are parks and sports fields only in a few cities. Tennis courts, for example, are found in only three places within the country. Reading material is scarce.

What do people do when they are not working? Mostly people just relax and hang out. You talk to friends, listen to other people talking to their friends, sip a cup of milk tea in the village tea shop and watch people walk by.

Maybe you lie down in a cool, shady spot and take a nap, or maybe just sit under a tree and do nothing, waiting for a friend to come by and to discuss the latest village gossip.

Above: **Bhaag-chaal is a form of Nepalese chess with pieces in the form of tigers and goats. Usually, though, stones are used as a substitute as people cannot afford to buy a set.**

Opposite: **At Namche Bazaar, the sale of clothes and food attract crowds of Sherpas to this once-a-week market.**

Left: **Soccer is regularly played in the more urban areas of Nepal but is not popular in the hills because of the lack of flat land.**

Going to the movies is a favorite pastime of Nepalese. They will sometimes pay three to four times the price for tickets to a popular movie on the black-market.

MOVIES

People in Nepal love to go to the movies. Every large town with electricity will have a theater of some kind. Movies are a great bargain: even the best seats are only about 30 cents. Most of the movies are from India and are in the Hindi language. Many Nepalese speak Hindi, which is very similar to Nepali.

Even the smallest understanding of Hindi is enough to enjoy the movies. The plots are simple and direct, villains are really bad and the heroes are all almost supermen.

Movies last about three hours and have a little bit of everything—tragedy, comedy, rock'em-sock'em fights and spectacular musical numbers, often switching from one to the other in seconds. The seats may be backless benches, the theater may be hot as an oven, and the projector bulb may blow every 10 minutes, but movies are still great entertainment.

Video is bringing movies to even the most remote villages. Porters will carry a TV, a VCR and a small generator for days through the hills, turning each village school hall into a temporary theater. The entire village will turn out to watch. For many, it is the first movie of any kind. At first they cannot even understand the images on the screen, but like us, they become critics quickly.

Kite flying is an exciting pastime for people of all ages, particularly around the Dasain Festival in fall.

TRADITIONAL PASTIMES AND SPORTS

With no money to spend on elaborate games or equipment, most Nepalese games only need what can be picked up from the ground to play.

One of the most popular children's game is *dhandi-biu* (stick and seed). A bat-like stick is used to flick the end of a small seed lying on the ground, flipping it into the air. The player tries to tap the seed twice whilst still in the air, and on the third time hit it as far as possible. The farthest hit wins.

Kite flying is another popular sport. Nepalese kites have no tails and control is very difficult. The kites are not just flown; once up in the air you look for another kite to fight with. The object is to use your own kite's string to snap the string of your opponent. During the kite flying season, the sky above towns will be dotted with kites swirling and dipping to gain an advantage. Rooftops are full of spectators young and old who cheer on their favorite. The streets are full of small boys chasing down the losers' kites as they float down to the ground.

Nepal's most famous game is called *baagh-chaal* (tiger and goats, played on what looks like a Chinese checkers board).The object of the game is for the tigers to eat up all the goats by jumping over them onto an open space, or for the goats to trap all the tigers by preventing the tigers from moving.

Nepalese children amuse themselves by playing a variety of games using stones or whatever else is at hand.

KABADDI

The traditional national sport is a game which originated in India called Kabaddi. Two teams face each other across a line on the ground. A player from **A** team rushes across the line and attempts to tag one of the players on **B** team, all the time saying "kabaddi." The players on **B** team attempt to avoid his tag, but when he does tag one of them, they rush to stop him from recrossing the line. If they can stop him till he runs out of breath and stops yelling "kabaddi," they win. He wins if he recrosses the line. There is another similar game for all-girl teams. National tournaments for both sexes are held every year.

MODERN SPORTS

Volleyball is the most popular sport in the hills because it does not require a large playing field. In the *terai* and larger valleys, soccer is also popular. There are several national club tournaments and teams from all over Asia are invited to take part. Cricket is played in some large towns.

In the 1988 Seoul Olympics, a Nepalese boxer won Nepal's first and only Olympic medal ever, a bronze. The martial arts, particularly tae kwon do, are becoming very popular and Nepalese players are now strong contestants in all-Asian competitions.

Because the game of volleyball needs only a small piece of flat land and little equipment, it is becoming very popular in Nepal.

Opposite: **The biggest one-day *mela* is held at Tribeni on the banks of the Narayani River. Over 100,000 people gather to bathe on the full moon of February.**

Right: **Gambling is a regular feature at the *mela*. Here, the men bet on which way the walnut shells will land when thrown.**

THE MELA

Strictly local festivals called *mela* are a main source of local entertainment and leisure. *Mela* are religious celebrations held annually. The date of the *mela* is based on the phase of the moon, usually at full moon or new moon, or half way between. Nothing much happens at the *mela* except that people have a good time.

They see friends from other villages, eat foods they cannot always find, and buy some clothes or jewelry. Men gamble, women gossip. Young people sing, dance, and court; and small children do not worry about bedtimes. These days, no one is surprised if a video and generator are carried in. A series of two or three movies will be shown non-stop for as long as there is fuel for the generator.

Mela can last between a day to several days. Each community in an area will have its own, providing entertainment at intervals throughout the year. Usually *mela* are held beside or near rivers or streams. People will walk for days to come to a good *mela*.

FESTIVALS

NEPAL HAS DOZENS OF FESTIVALS. If you include local festivals, it is safe to say that there is a festival every day somewhere in Nepal. Although there are some secular holidays, all the major holidays and festivals are based on some religious celebration.

Many are dedicated to the worship of a specific god or goddess. Shiva Raatri is dedicated to the Hindu god Shiva; but some have a more human emphasis. Bhai Tika, for example, is a festival between members of a family, and Tij is a festival for women only.

Because of the differences between Hindus and Buddhists, what is a festival for one group may mean nothing to another. Dasain, the biggest Hindu holiday, is nothing to Buddhists. Losar, New Year's Day and the year's biggest holiday for Himalayan people, is not celebrated by the rest of the population. Indra Jatra is only observed in the Kathmandu Valley.

Usually, each area will have its own festival once a year. These festivals are a combination of a religious celebration and a county fair. Overnight small stalls selling food and trinkets will spring up in an open field. People will walk all day, celebrate, eat, sing, dance and gamble all night, then walk back home the next day. The date for such *mela* depends on a particular phase of the moon in the same month each year. It is common to hold a *mela* under a full moon. The largest fair is the Tribeni Mela held under the full moon each February. Over 100,000 people gather for this one-day fair.

Opposite: **At the Raato Machhendranath festival, this woman seer waits for a customer. She is consulted for advice on suitable marriage dates and even for partners.**

Below: **A joker in the Gai Jatra Festival. During this event, people are given the opportunity to poke fun at just about anything.**

A FESTIVAL CALENDAR

The dates for festivals are determined using Nepal's lunar calendar and the dates change annually on the Gregorian. Calendar.

December–January	Seto Machhendranath The Holy Month of Magh
February–March	Shiva Raatri—Lord Shiva's Night
March–April	Baleju Jatra Ghora Jatra
April–May	Biskhet Jatra Mother's Day Raato Machhendranath Buddha Jayanti—Buddha's Birthday
May–June	Mani Rimdu
June–July	Tribhuvan Jayanti
July–August	Naga Panchami—Day of the Snakes Janai Purnima—the sacred thread
August–September	Gai Jatra Krishna Jayanti— Krishna's Birthday Father's Day Tij—Women's Festival
September–October	Indra Jatra Dasain Tihar
November–December	Sita Bibha Panchami Bala Chaturdasi

TIHAR—THE FESTIVAL OF LIGHTS

Tihar feels very much like Christmas. There are gifts, decorated houses lit at night, special foods, and even a special nocturnal visitor: Laxmi, goddess of wealth and good fortune.

Five animals are worshiped during Tihar. On the first day, housewives leave food out for crows. On the second day, dogs are given flower necklaces and *tika* and fed at a banquet. Cows, symbols of Laxmi, are bathed and garlanded on the third day, bullocks on the fourth, and people worship each other and themselves on the last.

At midnight of the third day, Laxmi, riding her owl, visits deserving houses. Homes are cleaned and tinsel and colored lights or oil lamps are placed everywhere. A path is painted and adorned with oil lamps from outside the door to inside the place where the home's valuables wait for the goddess's blessing. Beside the valuables are a burning lamp, some flowers and food for Laxmi. Excited children set off fireworks.

During the festival of Tihar, the cities and towns are ablaze with lights to guide the goddess of wealth to their homes.

Women of the neighborhood go singing from house to house and are rewarded with presents. On the following night, it is the men's turn.

On the fourth day, homes are lit again and Newars celebrate their New Year's Day. The fifth day is most important. All over Nepal, brothers travel to visit their sisters to receive *bhai tika* (brother's blessing). This blessing is so important that if a boy does not have a sister, a relative will act as a sister. In return for the blessing, the sister receives gifts of cloth and money.

TIJ—FESTIVAL FOR WOMEN

During the Festival of Tij, women dress in bright red *sari* after having their ritual bath in the river.

Even though it means fasting for at least a day, women in Nepal look forward to the three days of Tij, the only festival they can call their own. It is their only break from household duties. On the first day, women of the house eat a fine feast, sparing no expense as they must fast on the second day.

The fast replicates one done by Parbati as she prayed that Shiva would marry her. Shiva did marry her, and in return, Parbati promised any women who fasted would have a good marriage and many children.

All day, groups of women gather by rivers and streams. After bathing, they dress in their best clothes, usually a bright red *sari*, and worship Shiva. Then they gather with their friends and neighbors to sing and dance long into the night.

On the morning of the third day, each woman makes an offering of food to her husband and breaks her fast. A ritual bath ends the festival.

SHIVA RAATRI—SHIVA'S NIGHT

Each February, tens of thousands come to bathe in the Bagmati River at the point where it flows by Pashupati Temple in Kathmandu Valley. Devotees come from all over India and Nepal on the 14th day of the waning moon, the anniversary of a night long ago which Shiva spent here in meditation.

Shiva is said to have loved the spot so much, he returns on the same night each year to meditate. By spending the night in meditation and bathing at dawn, you gain great favor with the powerful Lord Shiva.

In February, the temperature may be 32 F and the water is freezing cold. Bathing is no easy thing to do. The woods near the temple becomes a huge campground, lit with the fires of thousands of pilgrims chanting and trying to keep warm through the long night.

At the first light of dawn, people start bathing in the icy river. They stand in line for hours to pour a little of the river water over a stone *lingam* (fertility symbol) representing Shiva.

People throng to bathe along the river of Pashu-pati Temple to celebrate Shiva Raatri.

RAATO MACHHENDRANATH

Each year, the great god Raato (red) Machhendra is taken from his temple, placed in a wagon topped by a 40-foot spire of pine-covered bamboo, and pulled through the narrow streets of Patan. Stops are made in each neighborhood to give all a chance to worship. The Raato Machhendra is believed to control the monsoon rains, so it is vital to keep him happy.

It can take a month to travel through the city. The wagon collides with houses, the spire threatens to fall over, wheels get stuck in gutters. Each neighborhood takes a turn in supplying the hundred or so men necessary to pull the wagon.

The climax comes in an open field where the king comes to display a sacred vest given ages ago by the Serpent King to the Raato Machhendra for safekeeping. The continued presence of the vest guarantees plenty of rain for the coming rice-planting season. Tens of thousands cheer as the king holds the vest high for all to see.

INDRA JATRA

The eight-day Indra Jatra is the main festival of the Kathmandu Valley. Long ago, Indra, the god of rain, came to the valley to steal some beautiful flowers he saw from high above. He was caught by the people and tied in heavy ropes like a common man. It was not until Indra's mother came to seek him and convinced the people of Indra's true identity that they released him. In return, she gave the people two gifts. She would take to heaven all those who died that year and she gave the valley the moist, foggy winter mornings that help moisten the crops even today.

Indra Jatra is also used to worship the terrible god, Bhairav, the destroyer. Every neighborhood puts a mask of this terrifying deity on display and worships him. The climax of this celebration begins at night when, from a large mask of Bhairav, rice beer flows out and crowds of young men wrestle for a drink.

During the festival, beautifully costumed and masked dancers wander through Kathmandu, re-enacting the search for Indra.

For three nights, Kumari, the living Goddess, is then drawn through the streets. On the second night, as thousands wait, the Kumari gives a *tika* to the king. This rite symbolizes the goddess's blessing on the king, and continued prosperity for the kingdom.

From the huge mouth of a Bhairav mask, rice beer is released. Somewhere in the flow is a small fish. To drink it is to have guaranteed prosperity for the next year.

Here we see elements of worship used during Dasain. The knife at the top is called a *kukri*.

DASAIN

Dasain is as important to Nepalese Hindus as Christmas is to Christians. All offices and stores close for most of this 11-day celebration. Nepalese will do anything they can to be home for it. All workers receive a bonus, usually one month's pay. Special foods are made and everyone receives a present of a new set of clothes.

Dasain celebrates the victory of good over evil, represented by the victory of the goddess Durga over the demon Mahisasura, who terrorized the earth in the form of a huge water buffalo. Durga, wife of Shiva, is pictured riding a tiger or lion, her dozen arms filled with the weapons she used to defeat Mahisasura, lying prostrate beneath her feet.

On the first day, each household plants barley seeds. On the ninth, each household sacrifices an animal (fowl, goats, or even a water buffalo) by slitting the throat or beheading it with a large *kukri*. The blood from the animals is dripped over all vehicles, from bicycles to jet planes, to insure Durga's protection for the coming year. The sacrifices are followed by a big feast.

The actual victory of Durga over the demon is celebrated on the tenth day. Everyone puts on the new clothes bought for Dasain and visits relatives and friends to exchange greetings and *tika* on this day of joy. On the eleventh day, the barley, which has grown into bright green sprouts, is distributed by the head of the house and worn on the head as a sign of blessing.

The Goddess Durga rides her tiger as she triumphs over evil. Nepalese celebrate her victory during Dasain, the biggest festival in Nepal.

THE KUMARI

The Kumari is believed to be the goddess Kanya Kumari in human form. The Kumari is chosen at the age of about four from the Sakya clan of gold and silversmiths.

Her body must have 32 special signs and cannot have any flaws or scars. She must identify items known only to the Kumari. Lastly, she must walk fearlessly through a dark room filled with men in demon masks and bloody buffalo heads. If she passes all that, she is the Kumari, the living goddess.

She moves into a palace, and while she lives like a queen in the palace, she is forbidden to leave except for a few special occasions. Even then, she is carried as her feet must never touch the ground.

She remains the Kumari until she loses blood either from a cut or upon reaching puberty. Then she returns to her own family, an ordinary person again.

BUDDHIST HOLIDAYS

LOSAR The most important festival in the Himalayan areas is Losar, or New Year's Day. It is a time for dressing up in new clothes, visiting family and friends, and lots of eating and drinking.

At Boudhanath near Kathmandu, big crowds string prayer flags from the stupa. A photo of the Dalai Lama, the spiritual leader of Tibetan Buddhists (and exiled secular leader of Tibet) is carried through the crowd.

At the climax, an exact moment determined by astrologers, everyone hurls handfuls of Tsampha flour (flour made from roasted barley) into the air, then at each other. Groups of people form long lines, arms over each other's shoulders, and dance in a slow shuffle.

BUDDHA JAYANTI On the full moon of April or early May, the birth of the Buddha is celebrated throughout Nepal's Buddhist community. People make trips to a monastery, where lamas hold special services, and there are feasts and visiting of friends and relatives. In Kathmandu, Swayambhu Temple is the center of the celebrations, with thousands climbing the 300 steep stairs to the top to worship at the many shrines around the stupa.

FESTIVALS OF THE FAMILY AND HOME

DASAIN and **BHAI TIKA** are festivals that combine the worship of a god and goddess with a celebration that strengthens family ties. There are several other festivals too which are mainly to strengthen the ties between family and home and primarily celebrated within the family.

MOTHER'S DAY, known as "aamaa-ko mukh herne din," literally meaning "see mother's face day." All children, even those that have married and moved away (usually daughters) return home. They present sweets, fruits and other gifts to their mother and bend down to touch their forehead to her feet as a sign of their respect. Mother places her hand on their forehead as a sign of blessing.

FATHER'S DAY, "Buaa-ko mukh herne din," is celebrated in much the same way as Mother's Day.

A picture of Krishna with the Serpent King behind him.

RAKSHA BANDHAN Sisters tie decorated silk threads around their brother's right wrist and give a *tika* as signs of sisterly affection and devotion. In return, their brother gives gifts and promises to look after them all his life.

NAGA PANCHAMI Houses in Nepal are usually built from clay bricks or mud and rock. It is common for the houses to collapse in the heavy monsoon rains. Nepalese blame this on the anger of the snake gods living in the ground beneath the house. To keep the snake gods happy, on Naga Panchami, every family fixes a picture of the Serpent King and his retainers above the home's main door. A bright red *tika* is given to the Serpent King's forehead, the snakes are prayed to and offerings of milk, honey, curd and rice are placed outside.

FOOD

WHEN TWO NEPALESE MEET on the road, the first question they will ask each other is, "*Bhaat khanu bhaeyo?*" (Have you eaten rice?) That shows how much importance Nepalese place on eating rice. Often, Nepalese use the word *khanaa* (food) when they are talking about *bhaat* (cooked rice). Rice is the food of choice, but in much of the country, having rice to eat is a luxury and a sign of wealth and status.

Rice can only grow at altitudes up to about 6,000 feet and needs lots of water. Most of the country cannot meet those conditions. Rice must be carried in on someone's back in many places, raising its price till many people can eat it only on special occasions.

Opposite: **A Nepalese feast fit for a king. Many Nepalese, though, will never be able to afford to eat such an expensive meal in all their lives.**

Below: **A group of Gurung women harvesting millet. Later, the millet grains will be ground to make bread, or fermented to produce liquor.**

Most people depend on other grains—wheat, corn and millet at the lower and middle altitudes, barley and buckwheat at the higher altitudes. The grain is ground into flour by hand or water-powered mill and boiled into a thick paste or cooked into a pancake-like bread called *roti*.

A classic Nepalese meal is *dal bhaat tarkaari* (lentil soup, rice, curried vegetables), which can be a very nutritious and satisfying meal. The lentils provide protein, rice is the carbohydrate and the vegetables provide vitamins and minerals. Meat is not a daily part of the meal; neither are eggs. Milk and curd are more common, but still not everyday food in most houses. *Achaar*, pickled vegetables, is a popular side dish.

Fiery red chilies are dried out in the sun. They will be blended with other spices to make curries.

FOOD CUSTOMS

Only eat with the right hand, your clean hand. It is important to wash your hand before you eat (and necessary after!).

To eat a Nepalese meal, pour some of the lentil soup over a portion of the rice. Mix the soup and rice, form it into a bite-size portion, and pop it in your mouth (all with your right hand). Take a bit of the vegetables, pickles, or whatever there is. *Dal bhaat tarkaari* eaten this way tastes better than when eaten Western-style.

Once you have eaten any food from a plate, never offer anything from that plate to someone else. All the food on the plate becomes *jutho* (contaminated) when you eat even the tiniest piece of anything. To offer it to another person is a huge insult. Any food not eaten is thrown to the animals. This taboo is not as strong with Himalayan people.

Meals are taken twice a day, in the mid-morning and in the evening before bedtime, with a simple snack in-between.

Hindus are forbidden from eating any beef by their religion.

Brahmins have many diet restrictions. They should not eat chicken, duck, buffalo, onion, leeks, mushrooms and tomatoes.

All foods are classified as hot and cold based on their effect on the body. Mango is hot, yogurt is cold. Cinnamon, cloves, pepper and nutmeg are *garam masala* (hot spices).

Water is usually drunk from a communal pitcher. If a person's mouth touches the pitcher, it becomes *jutho* and must be thrown out. People drink by pouring the water into their open mouth, swallowing at the same time.

Just before rice is placed on the plate, the plates are rinsed with water to clean them. A dry plate is considered unclean.

Nepalese do not eat dessert. After a meal they chew a piece of betel nut or a clove or cardamom.

Before serving rice, Nepalese throw a few grains of rice into the fire as an offering to the gods.

FOOD AND VEGETABLES

The main vegetable is potato, found almost everywhere. Spinach and squash are also common. Everyday vegetables like onions and carrots are extremely rare, except in major towns.

There are no refrigerators and no canned food. Some foods, like potatoes and onions, can be stored for long periods, but most foods spoil quickly. In the rural areas, vegetables are cooked as soon as they are picked. In the towns, people shop every day, buying whatever they plan on eating that day.

Meat is a rare treat, usually served on festive occasions. Mutton is the most common meat consumed. Before a goat is killed and butchered, the division of the meat will be arranged among families in the village. If not enough families are interested, the goat is not killed.

This simple vegetable stand along the sidewalk is filled with exotic fruits such as bananas, chilies and cherry tomatoes.

119

Milk is an important source of protein. It is never drunk cold, but is always boiled and served hot. Yogurt is also very popular. Often the milk or yogurt is poured over the rice and mixed with the rest of the food.

Curry in Nepal does not come bottled. The spices are ground together on a stone fresh for each meal, and each cook has his or her own recipe. Nepalese use any of the dozens of spices in the market or they grow it themselves: turmeric, cumin, coriander, cardamom, pepper, fennel, fenugreek, ginger, mustard seeds, even cloves, cinnamon, nutmeg or mace. Most people like their food hot and will throw a couple of red-hot chilies onto the grindstone, too.

A typical meal may consist of two or three of the following dishes: rice, lentil soup, curried vegetables, fried spinach, beans, yogurt or fried bread.

FOOD IN THE HIMALAYAN REGION

The food of the Himalayan area is based on several staples. One of them is tea. After the tea is brewed, it is poured in what looks like an old-fashioned butter churn. Butter and salt are added and churned in thoroughly. The salty, buttery tea is then poured into a jug and placed by the fire. The taste is strange at first, but it gets better with every cup and can quickly become a habit. Healthy and hearty, it is drunk throughout the day and offered immediately to any visitor.

Tsampa, roasted barley ground into flour, is the staple. The flour is often mixed with tea in a cup into a thick gruel or paste and eaten with the fingers. Sometimes it is made into a thick stew with potatoes and meat added. *Tsampa* is also made into thick *roti* and fried in butter.

The other staple is potatoes, boiled or baked in the fire's coals. A big plate of potatoes is a meal in itself, eaten by dipping them in a plate of

With no refrigeration, dried goods are a staple food of Nepalese diet. This store has all kinds of dried beans, lentils and vegetables.

salt ground together with hot chilies.

Meat is also common; the dry, cold climate preserves it for months. Their Buddhist religion allows them to eat meat, but it forbids them from killing any animal. Northern folks often hire people from the Middle Hills to come and slaughter the animals for them.

A young man pouring *chhang* or rice beer into a bucket.

THE NATIONAL DRINK

Tea is Nepal's national drink. In Nepalese tea, your choices for what to add go far beyond sugar and milk or lemon. Nepalese add whatever spices they have handy—ginger, cloves, cinnamon, cinnamon leaves and cardamom are common additions to the teapot. Nepalese like their tea sweet, spicy and milky. If there is no sugar, a pinch of salt is added to each cup.

On cold winter mornings, Nepalese will brew raw ginger or ground black pepper in their milk tea. It is hard to imagine a better drink on a cold winter morning than hot, milky tea spiced with pepper or ginger.

To make Nepalese tea, mix equal parts of milk and water in a pot, throw in your favorite spices and bring to a boil. After boiling a few minutes, add the tea (Nepalese tea comes in loose powder form; tea bags are unknown) and boil for another minute or two. Then strain into a 6-ounce glass, not a cup or mug, and drink. Sugar can be added anytime while making it. The tea should be sweet.

LIQUOR

It is illegal to make liquor in Nepal, but it would be the rare house indeed (except for high-caste Hindus) that did not. In the Middle Hills and Himalayan areas, tea and sugar may be rare, and the morning may start instead with a glass of warmed *raksi*.

There are two main types of liquor. *Chhang* is a fermented beer-like drink. Almost always made from rice, it is a meal in itself.

Raksi is the more common drink. It is a distilled drink made from any type of grain, but usually from millet. Water is added again after it has been distilled. It is usually drunk after warming it, and some butter and a few grains of roasted rice are sometimes added to give it more flavor.

Drinking is a favorite social institution. Drink is usually taken with a small plate of snacks, meat, if possible. Eating and drinking are separate. The meal is not eaten until drinking is finished, which means the meal may be delayed until 10 or 11 at night. After eating, the evening is finished and everyone goes home or heads for bed.

A favorite drink in the east is *thoumba*. Fermented millet is placed in a pitcher, hot water is added and the concoction sipped through a bamboo straw. Water can be added two or three times and one pitcher may last for hours of conversation.

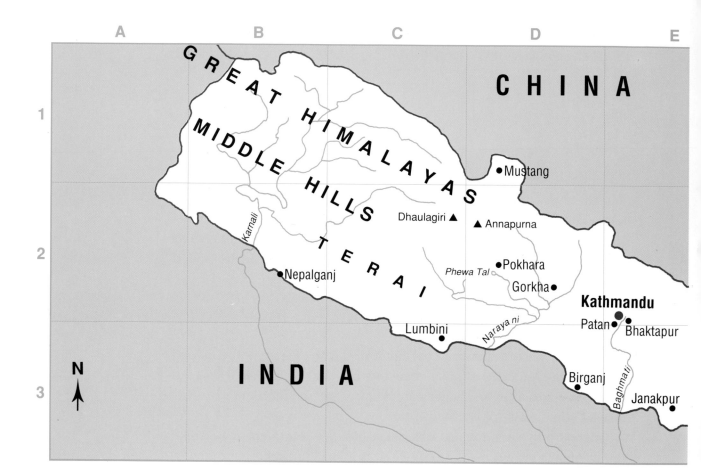

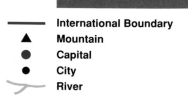

International Boundary
▲ Mountain
● Capital
● City
River

NEPAL

F   G

▲ Mount Everest

GREAT HIMALAYAS

BHUTAN

SIKKIM

MIDDLE HILLS

Kosi

TERAI

●Biratnagar

BANGLADESH

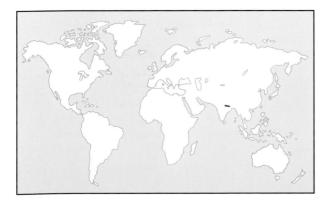

QUICK NOTES

Land Area
56,139 square miles

Population
18 million

Capital City
Kathmandu

Major Rivers
Mechi, Sapt Kosi, Tamur, Arun, Dudh Kosi, Sun Kosi, Trishuli, Marsyandi, Buri Gandaki, Kali Gandaki, Narayani, Karnali, Seti, Mahakali

Major Lakes
Phewa, Rara

Highest Point
Mount Everest, also called Sagarmatha 29,028 feet the highest point on Earth

Climate
Varies from semi-tropical in the south to arctic in the north

Religions
Hinduism 90%, Buddhism 8%, Islam 2%

Languages
Nepali is the official language, but is the mother tongue for only about 50% of the population; about 12 other major languages; English is also understood by some

Major Ethnic Groups
Caste Hindus; and dozens of other tribal groups, the largest being Tamangs, Gurungs, Magars, Rais, Limbus, Sherpas, Tharus, Newars

Currency
Nepalese Rupee
(US$1.00 = 30 Rupees)

Major Exports
Woolen carpets, jute, tea

National Flower
Rhododendron

Important Figures in Nepal's History
Gunakamadeva—10th century king, founder of Kathmandu
Jayasthiti Malla—14th century king, made the caste system law
Yaksha Malla—15th century king, patron of the arts
Prithivinarayan Shah—founder of Nepal, conquered the Kathmandu valley in 1768
Jung Bahadur Rana—led the Rana coup in 1847, established the Rana dynasty
B.P. Koirala—led the fight for democracy, first elected prime minister in 1961
King Tribhuvan—retook power from the Ranas in 1951
King Mahendra—dissolved parliament in 1961, re-established absolute monarchy
King Birendra—returned power to the people in 1990, currently the constitutional monarch of Nepal

GLOSSARY

bhaat	Cooked rice.
daal	A thick lentil soup, served at almost every meal.
kukri	The Nepalese national knife with a characteristic curved blade.
Namaste	The traditional greeting and farewell, spoken with hands clasped together.
puja	Worshiping a Hindu deity.
prasad	The blessing, usually some food and flowers received after finishing a *puja*.
stupa	A traditional Buddhist structure, a hemispheric mound topped with a spire.
thangka	Tibetan religious paintings with Buddhist themes, usually done on small- or medium-sized paper.
tika	A mark of blessing on the forehead, usually made with red powder.
Vedas	The Hindu scriptures dating back to about 2000 B.C.

BIBLIOGRAPHY

Aung San, Suu Kyi.: *Nepal,* Chelsea House, New York, 1988
De Cherisey, Christine.: *My Village in Nepal*, Silver Burdett, Englewood Cliffs, N.J. 1985
Goodman, Jim.: *Kathmandu*, Times Editions, Singapore, 1988
Hagen, Toni.: *Nepal: The Kingdom of the Himalayas*, Kummerly and Frey, 1971
Lye, Keith.: *Take a trip to Nepal*, Franklin Watts, New York, 1988
Watanabe, Hitobe.: *Children of the World: Nepal*, Gareth Stevens, Milwaukee, 1987

INDEX